RESOURCES *for* DEACONS

Love Expressed through Mercy Ministries

Timothy J. Keller

Presbyterian Church in America Committee on Discipleship Ministries
Lawrenceville, Georgia

© PCA Committee on Discipleship Ministries
ISBN: 0-9703541-6-9

Table of Contents

Preface 5
The High Calling of Deacon — Dr. George C. Fuller 7

Biblical Basics for Diaconal Ministry

The Mandate for Mercy Ministry 15
The Definition and Dynamic of Mercy Ministry 18
Two Common Objections to the Ministry of Mercy 21
Five Common Questions on Evaluating Need 23
The Three "Levels" of Mercy 25

Organizing for Diaconal Ministry

The Biblical Office of Deacon 29
Two Proposals for Committees of the Diaconate 32
Evaluation of Present Diaconal Ministry 35
Diaconal Spiritual Gifts 37
Diaconal Ministry and Church Growth 39
Steps for Mobilizing a Church Mercy Ministry 42
Surveying Your Community for Diaconal Needs 44
Guidelines for a Deacons' Fund 48
The Service Bank: By-laws 50
"Service-Talent Bank" Survey 52
Outline for Mission Groups 54
The Ministry of Referral 56
Mercy Ministry Planning Worksheet 59
Presbytery Diaconal Associations 61

Needs and Programs for Diaconal Ministry

Programs for the Poor 65
Resettling Refugees — Dr. John H. Skilton 71
Needs of the Elderly 74
Programs for the Elderly 81
Nursing Home Ministry 84
Programs for Disadvantaged Children 86
Helping Parents With Their Parenting 89
A Flow Chart for Helping Unwed Mothers 92
Prisoners: Their Problems and the Biblical Solution 95
Guide for Visiting the Sick 97
Programs for the Handicapped 104
Ministry in Disaster 106

Table of Contents

Casework in Diaconal Ministry

Two Kinds of Poverty 109
Assessing Mercy Needs 111
Strategies for Adequate Employment 114
An Outline for Vocational Counseling 115
An Outline for Financial Counseling 117
How to Help Someone Face Suffering 119
Developing a Ministry Plan 122
Two Case Studies 126

Preface

In 1983 the National Presbyterian and Reformed Fellowship published **A Sourcebook of Mercy for Deacons** edited by George C. Fuller and Timothy Keller. That notebook is foundation for this manual. Dr. Keller is responsible for the diaconal ministry program in the Presbyterian Church in America and is a staff member of Mission to North America. He is also on the faculty of Westminster Theological Seminary assisting in the practical theology department plus coordinating the Doctor of Ministry program.

Approximately half of the articles in this manual are articles from the **Sourcebook**. Combined with the completely new articles, Dr. Keller has developed a "think tank" source for mercy ministries in local churches.

There are forty brief articles in this manual. Each deals with a specific aspect of diaconal or mercy ministries. Most of the articles are very brief and basic. They are designed to act as springboards for interested members who can use each one to develop a plan of action for implementation in the local church.

We suggest that each church use this manual as a study in its entirety. Then in light of the present situation in your church and community we encourage you to begin to set up priorities that will most reflect your understanding of God's will for you and your church at this point in time.

Don't be overwhelmed by the tremendous volume of ideas and ministries suggested. The tendency might be to put it aside. To avoid such a procedure prioritizing your opportunities would be an invaluable step.

Much that comes under the category of mercy ministry requires an education and training process that will help your people see the needs and be trained to be part of that vital ministry.

You will find this manual to be a gold mine of ideas and resources in this much neglected part of the Christian ministry. It is divided into four major areas. You could study the entire manual, or select one major group at a time or even one section.

Our desire in offering this manual to the churches of the Presbyterian Church in America is that they will be encouraged to become more aware of and involved in mercy ministry. The entire Reformed and Evangelical world has been, at least for the past ten years, attempting to look seriously at the social implications and applications of the gospel.

If the PCA is to be on God's cutting edge and implementing a ministry that is effectively carrying out God's purpose, mercy ministry must be a vital part.

We commend to you this manual and its many ideas for ministry to those in need.

Charles Dunahoo

The High Calling of Deacon

George C. Fuller

Just north of Hyde Park and overlooking the Hudson valley stands the palatial Vanderbilt mansion. During the winter months two people lived here, served by over twenty maids, butlers, chauffers, groundskeepers, cooks and servants. Vanderbilt money was plentiful and powerful. Measured against the standards of past and present societies, the Vanderbilts "had it made." Wealthy, powerful, they sat where others have longed to be.

Jesus told his disciples, "You know that the rulers of the Gentiles lord it over them, and their great men exercise authority over them."

The world has always measured greatness by the standard of service, not service a person gives, but that which he receives. In business a man or woman is often judged successful if many people "report to him." Happiness and success is then to be found at the top of the pyramid. At the bottom is misery and drudgery.

Plato said, "How can a man be happy when he has to serve someone?" For the Greeks, menial "service" was not dignified, surely not to be sought as a way of life.

But Jesus changed all that, radically reversing the world's standards. He did not make subtle changes or adjustments in a well-entrenched system. He turned the whole thing upside down, making, as it were, the first last and the last first.

That kind of change does not allow for compromise. Choice is necessary, and only between two options. Greatness in life, achievements is measured by the world's standard, "service received," or by the standard of Jesus: "service given."

How does someone reverse a standard whose acceptance has been so nearly universal among all people and throughout all centuries, perhaps especially in our present world? First, know that we are not talking about "someone"; we're talking about Jesus. More than Jesus the man, he is Jesus the Creator, Jesus the Son, Jesus the Lord. This world owes its beginning and its continuance to him and his power. The one who seeks to overturn the standards of a world that exalts men of power is himself King of kings and Lord of lords. With God the Father and God the Holy Spirit he is alone at the top of the pyramid; in fact, he is above the entire pyramid. So the precise question is: How does the Lord of glory set forth in a world of sin standards that utterly contradict its life-style, begun in Adam and continued to this day?

He does it by demonstration. He "deacons." Place high value on that word; it rises from the heart of the gospel. The Greek word meant to "serve at tables," and by extension, "to render humble, menial service for the benefit of others," Jesus said. "The Son of man came not to be served, but to serve."

That's the word: "I came not to be 'deaconed,' but to 'deacon'." For Jesus, "deaconing" meant giving sight to blind eyes, hearing to deaf ears, comfort to afflicted hearts, strength to weak legs, deliverance to tormented souls. He washed the disciples' feet. No wonder they were confused; their and the world's value system was being challenged. He endured capital punishment, emotional and spiritual agony beyond our comprehension, and not for any crime he had committed. He did it for others; he "deaconed."

If Jesus had not taken upon himself the "form of a servant," if the Lord of glory had not also "humbled himself and become obedient unto death, even death on a cross," the world's standard would be unchallenged. Not only would we be without his supreme example, as the one who though Lord of all became servant of all, we would also be deprived of his essential power. Having endured, suffered, died, Jesus was then raised, powerful, victorious, triumphant, now to live in and through his people. He is the "deacon," our ultimate example, and in his fulfilling of that charge from God is power for his people, his body on earth, to do his ministry.

The relationship between what Jesus did for us and what he does through us lies in the depths of his love. "God shows his love for us in that while we were yet sinners Christ died for us." Jesus' love for us is love for sinners. A righteous, pure, holy God loves that which is unclean, impure, unholy. He loves us in spite of what we are. To say of such love that it is unusual is an understatement; it is absolutely unique. He loves the unlovely, the unlovable, who have rejected him and his mercy. He loves them anyway and brings them to himself.

"If God so loved us, we also ought to love one another." The same kind of love with which the Christian was loved becomes his, namely, love for the unlovely, the unlovable, the dirty, the unclean. The love that Jesus demonstrated on the cross accomplishes our salvation, but it also gives us power for ministry. As no other person has every done, he "deaconed" on the cross. "He came not to be served, but to serve, and to give his life a ransom for many." In his diaconate, his ministry as deacon, there is the only hope for our diaconate, our ministry as deacons.

But Jesus does more than demonstrate the office of deacon and empower his people to fulfill that calling. He demands diaconal ministry from his people because they belong to him, whose life was marked by total self-giving and service. The New Testament calls his people "douloi" and "diakonoi," "slaves" and "waiters." As deacons, menial servants, they render service to God (II Cor. 6:4), to Christ (Jn. 12:26), to the new covenant (II Cor. 3:6), to the gospel (Eph. 3:7), to their fellow disciples (Mk. 10:43). Those who have his yoke placed upon them are commanded, "love your neighbor" or "love your enemy." I do not need to remind you that the entire New Testament makes clear that love which stops short of practical help is "in word only" or simply "with the tongue," a denial of the Lord we serve. The Reformers reminded us that absence of obedience is a sign of "no faith," "no salvation."

By example Jesus leads his people into diaconal ministry. In his death and resurrection he empowers them for this task. By command he calls them to obedient service. All that a deacon must do must be based on the diaconal ministry of his Lord and Savior. Our ministry of service is possible and is required, because Jesus came in the form of a servant.

The Reformation taught the priesthood of all believers; individual Christians have direct access to God through Christ. If we all share that privilege, if we are all priests, then we also all share responsibility for ministry. We are all deacons, ministers, servants, table-waiters to the benefit of each other, the world and to the glory of God. Such service is not optional. Empowered by the cross and resurrection of Jesus, it is commanded by Jesus. Cross-kind of love, cross-kind of service is characteristic of new life, the new view of greatness.

At the same time Scripture makes clear that certain people, properly chosen and elected, have special responsibility for diaconal ministry. Paul addressed his letter to the Philippians to "All the saints in Christ Jesus who are at Philippi, with the bishops and deacons." This greeting makes clear that the office was established early and that it stood in close relationship to the office of "bishop" or "elder."

In I Timothy 3:8-12, just after a challenge to "bishops," Paul sets forth qualifications for the high office of "deacon": "Deacons likewise must be serious, not double-tongued, not addicted to much wine, not greedy for gain; they must hold the mystery of the faith with a clear conscience. And let them also be tested first; then if they prove themselves blameless, let them serve as deacons. The women likewise must be serious, no slanderers, but temperate, faithful in all things. Let deacons be married only once, and let them manage their children and their households well; for those who serve well as deacons gain a good standing for themselves and also great confidence in the faith which is in Christ Jesus."

I Timothy 3 reveals that elders and deacons must share many qualities. Significantly, the elder must be "apt to teach," a quality not required of the deacon. The deacon, on the other hand, is not to be "double-tongued, not greedy for gain," qualities appropriate for all Christians, including elders, but specifically mentioned with regard to deacons. Deacons must exercise special mastery over their tongues. Hear James: "And the tongue is a fire. The tongue is an unrighteous world among our members, staining the whole body, setting on fire the cycle of nature, and set on fire by hell." Not extreme language in the light of damage done to us and by us, by words improperly spoken: lies, exaggerations, inuendo, gossip, betrayal. The deacon is not a teacher; basically that is elder's work. But the deacon is going to be involved in the lives of people, intimately involved; so he had better have his tongue under control.

These special qualifications give us insight into the nature of deacon's work. If all there is to being a deacon revolves around flowers and fruit baskets and the quick drop-off and pick-up of sermon tapes, these characteristics do not have special importance. But if indeed the deacon is going to meet people at their deep levels of need, if he is going to know people who hunger, thirst, who long for a friend, who need help of all kinds, then he needs special control of his tongue (and his ear) and special sensitivity with regard to money.

The duties of deacons in Presbyterian and Reformed churches are often derived from Acts 6. During the earliest church development (Acts 1-5) the apostles had maintained direct oversight over all the church's life, and done so under authority from the Lord himself. At Chapter 6, however, some believers with Greek background felt that their widows were being neglected in the daily distribution of food among the needy Christians. The Apostles gathered the Christians and urged them to pick seven of their number, so that (1) this duty might be properly done and (2) the apostles might be free to devote themselves to prayer and the ministry of the Word. Deacons today should expect therefore that their task is (1) to help people with various kinds of needs and (2) to relieve elders of these and other tasks that detract from their concentration on "prayer and the ministry of the Word." If, as a matter of fact, deacons did the task well, many sessions might find themselves with shorter agendas. Perhaps sensing that "risk," elders, "teaching" and "ruling" may be reluctant to allow deacons to fulfill their own high calling.

After the deacons had been appointed, the apostles continued to have active interest in ministry to the poor, the widows and others with needs (Acts 11:30). No Christian, not even an apostle, can give away his or her responsibility for the poor and the needy, the deprived and the dispossessed. You can't give it to your denominational headquarters or to your local board of deacons. Deacons therefore have an important responsibility in today's accelerated world. They must organize the ministry of mercy. They must become God's channel for mobilizing the members of his church to minister in the lives of others. When deacons see their role as that of activating the ministry of mercy by all the people of God, by the whole church, they have taken the first step toward multiplication of blessing in the lives of extended multitudes of suffering people.

The deacons also had high interest in other aspects of the gospel ministry after their appointment. Appointed in Acts 6 as a deacon, Stephen dies in Acts 7, the first Christian martyr. Philip, also one of the original seven, was "Philip, the evangelist," engaging in personal and mass evangelism (Acts 8). Today's deacon can trace his roots back to rich blood, some of which flowed in sacrificial service.

The office of deacon is a high calling under Jesus Christ. It is not a training ground for elders, although some deacons later become elders. It is not a secondary office; it is not unimportant. It is absolutely critical to the life of the church, in spite of often being ignored. The framers of the Westminster Confession of Faith discussed for months the duties of elders and the power of presbyteries, but concluded the subject of deacon in one day. Some Presbyterian churches today have disbanded their boards of deacons or reduced them to roles of money-gathering and grounds-keeping. What a tragedy that in a world filled with desperate people the church has so often lacked alert, creative, devoted deacons to challenge it and drive it by example and vision to responsive love.

J.K.S. Reid has written an article entitled "Diakonis in the Thought of Calvin," in a book called **Service in Christ** (London: Epworth Press, 1966). Reid affirmed: "It is difficult to imagine any single thing that would by itself do more to revive the church today than a recovered sense of this emphasis so typical of Calvin, that ministry means ministry. The legalism that formalizes ministry into a rank and neglects its essential character of service infects all churches." Reid makes clear that it was not the unimportance of the "care of widows" that caused it to be delegated; it was in fact its critical role in gospel ministry. The apostles simply did not have time or energy for two necessary and demanding ministries, the ministry of the Word and the ministry of mercy. To denigrate the high office of deacon is practical heresy.

The low estate of the office of deacon today is what we brought upon it, not what God intended. "When during World War II the Netherlands were occupied by Germans the deacons of the Dutch Reformed Church assumed the care for the politically persecuted, supplying food and providing secret refuge. Realizing what was happening, the Germans decreed that the elective office of deacon should be eliminated. The Reformed Synod on 17 July 1941 resolved: 'Whoever touches the diaconate interfers with what Christ has ordained as the task of the church . . . Whoever lays hands on *diakonia* lays hands on worship!' The Germans backed down" (Frederick Herzog, **Service in Christ,** p. 147). And we relegate our board of deacons to the past or to trivial roles, hardly essential to the kingdom ministry! The time is always proper to challenge deacons to their high calling; no time is better than right now.

We have seen that (1) Jesus demonstrates diaconal ministry uniquely, and that he also requires Christians to express diaconal love and concern. We have found that (2) the New Testament refers to specific officers in the church, called deacons, with necessary qualifications for office and tasks to fulfill. And we have learned that (3) deacons ought not to define their duties too narrowly and certainly ought to have the highest regard for the significance and importance of their office in God's plan for service and ministry in a needy and dying world.

What, then, does the deacon do? He ministers in the name of Jesus among lonely, sick, elderly, orphaned, widowed, dying, poor and deprived people. Some Christians have maintained that the board of deacons only has responsibility under God to minister to needy people within the church. There is, of course, pharisaic danger in even raising this question. The lawyer asked Jesus, "And who is my neighbor?", which, being interpreted, is "To whom should I show love?" or "How big should my neighborhood be?" "What are the geographical, physical limits for love?" The lawyer asked a question that rabbis had difficulty answering. Were they to love only other pharisees, or pious Jews, or all Jews, surely not Samaritans, not gentiles, certainly not enemies. But Jesus made clear that the critical issue is whether or not his would-be disciple is himself a neighbor to any with whom he or she comes into contact.

Churches whose board of deacons is charged with ministry only among its own people should at least note the warning of W. A. Whitehouse, ". . . a self-contained expression of diaconal service within the fellowship of the church has no witnessing power and is spoiled in its very character by a taint akin to incest." Perhaps the prevailing poverty among the early Christians demanded that special attention be directed to the pressing needs of brothers and sisters. Boards of deacons who believe that their field of ministry is within the limitations of the church can have rich and useful ministry, as they identify intimately with the needs of their congregation and begin to learn from Christians in neighboring communities who may be able to teach them how to minister to racially oppressed or poverty-burdened members of God's family.

So what does the deacon do? The specific answer is determined by the nature of the neighborhood. As Christians emerge from the protective comfort of their churches, they may find lonely people in boarding houses; poor people without food; young people with absentee parents; nursing-homed people without visitors (one nurse estimated that eighty per cent of the people in Pittsburgh's nursing homes never receive a visit from anyone); confused people without hope.

The board of deacons ought to seek involvement of the entire congregation in the ministry of mercy. A board of deacons, functioning properly, will give creative attention to the neighborhood in which it is called of God to function, but it will bring the same kind of creativity to the devising of a plan to give every member of its congregation clear opportunity for ministry to others. The apostles, even after the appointment of the "seven," continued to minister to people in need. How tragic to withhold that privilege from many Christians who simply wait for direction.

In our complex society the church, or at least individual Christians, must give attention to the "large" problems. Poverty will not diminish until its causes are mollified. Food for a hungry person is a necessary ministry, but the grain fields that have become dust bowls need attention also. The Reformers sought to aid hungry beggars, symptoms of an ailing society, but they also took aim at the basic problem. "Calvin . . . took the initiative of suggesting the setting up of the silk industry at Geneva to absorb surplus labor and to make possible the ending of begging" (G. W. Bromiley, **Service in Christ**, p. 111).

The problems of our cities need study, reflection, prayer. What Alan A. Brash (**Service in Christ,** pp. 206-207) wrote of Asian cities might be said of our cities also: "The churches have not really grappled seriously with the problems of the city. They have passed out their resources in sideline acts of organized mercy which, however commendable, have not touched the heart of the matter. Such charitable service has made little or no impact on the shape of the city itself, nor on its hectic rush to shame or glory. The dimensions of the problem have frozen the church into inaction." The disfavor that many of us have toward the pronouncements and postures of many church bodies on varied political matters ought not to prohibit us from seeking wisdom for positive contribution in world affairs when survival is at stake. (At the very last the board of deacons might ask for authority to sponsor the annual drive for funds for hunger, in an effort to bring that offering above the level of a collective pittance.)

And what happens when deacons fulfill their biblical mandate, when a church becomes a functioning community of service? For one thing, Christians become bound to one another as never before. John Calvin said, "The ministry of men . . . is a principle bond by which believers are kept together in one body" (IV, iii, 2).

A second result of an active diaconal ministry will be that we will have given the proper response to Jesus' diaconal ministry on our behalf. He served: we serve. Really, he serves through his body, the church, us. Without the ministry of mercy, the body is so incomplete. As though without an arm, a leg, the church seeks to stand, walk, run, but falls in confusion and uncertainty. In diaconal ministry we work out the salvation of the Lord with fear and trembling, until we see how that great gift touches everything and everybody that we touch. At every point of contact with his body the world sees and senses the love of God in Christ Jesus, love which commends and commands a ministry of mercy, diaconal ministry.

A third result is that we shall remove hypocrisy from our intercessory prayer. We shall be delivered from praying for the needs of others, while ignoring opportunities to minister to those in need. Our deeds to men will be brought into conformity with our words to God. Perhaps it should also be said at this point that the deacons might be specialists in intercessory prayer, not only praying themselves, but sharing with the congregation situations calling for prayerful attention.

A result hardly mentioned so far is that people will be helped. The evidence that Jesus offered to John's disciples that he was in fact the Christ was that the blind were seeing, the lame walking, lepers being cleansed, the deaf hearing and the gospel being preached to the poor. People were "being ministered unto," which is what he came to do. People were being helped, physically and spiritually, which is what it's all about for him and for his body.

"Deaconing" is a great Christian vocation. Under Christ's Lordship we can serve as successors of those who had the high privilege of ministering to him. After Jesus' temptation, "the angels came and ministered (deaconed) to him." After Jesus healed Peter's mother-in-law, "she rose and served (deaconed) him." High, holy privilege; to serve Jesus in person. At the cross stood women watching, "There were also many women there, looking on from afar, who had followed Jesus from Galilee, ministering (deaconing) to him, among whom were Mary Magdalene, and Mary the mother of James and Joseph, and mother of the sons of Zebedee." What blessed opportunity, to serve Jesus himself.

How tragic when the church does not heed the opportunity, respond to the call, to minister to Jesus in person, to serve the Lord himself. Christians, don't give up your birthright, your right by birth, the heritage of highest service. Deacons, don't retreat from God's high calling.

RESOURCES FOR DEACONS

Biblical Basics For Diaconal Ministry

The Mandate for Mercy Ministry

(A Biblical Survey)

I. **The Creation**
Adam is charged to subdue and have dominion over all of nature (Gen. 1:28). He is, therefore, to subdue both spiritual and material creation to the rule of God. God's servants are to be as concerned to subdue physical disorder and meet physical needs as to subdue spiritual disorder and meet spiritual needs. Both ministries are basic to covenant service of the Lord.

II. **The Fall of Man**
When Adam sins, nature is no longer our willing servant. Sickness, death, hunger, exposure, etc., enter our existence (Gen. 3:17ff. - "cursed is the ground . . . painful toil . . . to dust you will return"). Immediately after the fall we see the need to "clothe the naked." Both ministries are basic to covenant service of the Lord.

III. **The Patriarchal Period**
Job knew that God required mercy to the poor and needy (Job 29:15-16; 31:16-23). Sodom was destroyed for its unwillingness to care for the poor (Ezek. 16:49). Joseph "blessed the nations" (Gen. 12:3) by carrying out massive hunger relief as a civil magistrate (Gen. 47:53-57).

IV. **Early Israel**
God intends that there be no permanent poverty in his covenant community. (Deut. 15:4-5 - "there will be no poor among you . . . if you obey the voice of the Lord your God.") God legislates:

A. Social relief laws. The ordained ministry is to distribute tithes to the poor (Deut. 14:28-29). Individuals are to give to their poor

15

kindred (Lev. 25:25) and neighbors (Lev. 25:35-38) *until their need is gone* (Deut. 15:8, 10). This is not just spot relief.
- B. Economic development laws. When a slave is freed from debt he was to be given tools and grain to become self-sufficient (Deut. 15:12-15). Every 50 years all land was to return to the original family allotments, so as to continually give the needy the "capital" to become self-sufficient (Lev. 25).
- C. Social structures and institutions were established to protect the poor. The sabbath year cancelled all debts every seventh year (Deut. 15:11ff). The jubilee law (Lev. 25) returned land. Fair wages and business practices were regulated by law (Lev. 19:13, 35-37).

V. Later Israel

The prophets condemned Israel for neglecting the laws that protected the poor (Isa. 5:8-9; 3:11-26; Amos 6:4-7). The prophets taught that true heart religion is always marked by sensitivity to the poor (Isa. 1:10-17, 58:3-11).

VI. The Coming of Christ

- A. Jesus sees the proof of his Messiahship in his healing of the sick and preaching to the poor (Matt. 11:1-6).
- B. Jesus calls all his followers to be "deacons." *Diakones* means to meet the humblest, most basic needs of others (Luke 22:24-30). It means to meet physical needs in Matthew 25:44; 27:55; Luke 8:3. On judgment day, the reality of our faith will be tested by our deaconing of the poor (Matt. 25:44-46), since mercy is the natural response to the grace of God (Luke 6:35-36).
- C. Jesus associates and involves himself with the diseased and the outcasts. When confronted with these associations he calls people to the ministry of mercy (Matt. 12:7).

VII. The Church

The social righteousness demanded of the new Covenant community exceeds even the social legislation of the old.
- A. We are to give to the poor till his need is gone (I John 3:16-17 echoes Deut. 15:7-8).
- B. Ordained officers ("deacons") distribute to the poor as did the priests (Acts 6:1-7, see v. 7).
- C. Wealth within the community is given away to the "leveling" of lifestyles of all Christians (II Cor. 8:13-14 and Acts 4:32-37).

VIII. Summary

- A. Jesus is the true Adam (Rom. 5:15-21) who is subduing all creation to God (Eph. 1:9-10). So we are co-workers in bringing all nature into subjection to Christ (Matt. 28:18-20).

B. Jesus is the true High Priest (Heb. 4:14-16) who shows mercy to the needy. So we are royal priests (I Peter 2:9-10) whose deeds of mercy are sacrifices to God (Heb. 13:3-16).
C. Jesus is the great Deacon (Rom. 15:8) who identifies with the poor (II Cor. 8:9) and pours himself out in costly service (Mark 10:45). So we are deacons, who wash each others feet in humble service (Matt. 20:26-28; Gal. 6:10).

DISCUSSION QUESTIONS:
1. "The activity of 'deaconing' includes both an attitude and an action." Define that statement biblically.
2. Does your church "look down" at sins of personal unrighteousness (adultery, drunkeness) but overlook sins of social unrighteousness (greed, a luxury-loving spirit, etc.)? What attitude did the prophets have about those two categories of sin?

The Definition and Dynamic of Mercy Ministry

I. **The Definition of Mercy Ministry**
   Diaconal or mercy ministry is the meeting of human needs through deeds.
   A. Human needs are the focus of diaconal service.
      1. An illustrative list of such needs is provided by Jesus in Matthew 25:35-36. It includes food, shelter, and medical treatment. These needs are physical-economic in nature, but also implied is the need for a listening ear, kindness, and friendship ("I was a stranger and you welcomed me . . . I was in prison and you came to me.").
      2. What are "human needs"? They have these characteristics in common:
         a. They are needs which take no spiritual discernment to see in oneself or in others. They are "felt" needs. The world can understand what we are doing when they see us meeting them. For this reason, our deeds of mercy have an impact on the world (Matt. 5:16).
         b. They are needs which are not directly met when a person comes to Christ or grows in Christ. A man who is born again will starve to death as quickly as a non-Christian.
   B. Human needs are met primarily through deeds, rather than words.
      1. The Bible tells us Jesus was mighty in word and deed (Luke 24:19). Therefore, the ministry of the church is also "two-pronged." Spiritual gifts divide basically into two categories: word-gifts (e.g. exhortation, teaching, evangelism) and deed gifts (e.g. mercy, service, helps, administration). See I Peter 4:10. The church even has two permanent classes of officers to oversee each "prong" of the ministry. Elders supervise the ministry of the word while deacons coordinate the ministry of deeds (cf. Acts 6:1-6).
      2. Human needs are met through actions more than through words. James even warns us against doing word ministry when deed ministry is called for (Jas. 2:15-16). However, word and deed should not be separated. Diaconal service should be accompanied by both words of comfort (see Luke 7:13) and the proclamation of the gospel (see John 9:1-38).

II. **The Dynamic of Mercy Ministry**
    True mercy ministry is motivated by a grasp of the richness and depth of the grace of God toward undeserving sinners.

A. Diaconal or mercy ministry is costly. It is expensive financially and emotionally. It is time consuming. In the secular social work field there is a significant problem with "burnout" among workers. Where can Christians get the motivation to begin and persevere in this costly ministry?
B. There is a dynamic for mercy ministry — a powerful, spiritual energy which moves us to service. It is a deep heart-felt understanding of the grace of God.
    1. The dynamic is seen in Matthew 18:23-35. Jesus tells of a king who forgave a servant an infinite debt. The servant will not, in turn, forgive a fellow servant his debt. In anger, the king asks the first servant, "Should not you have had mercy on your fellow servant, as I had mercy on you?" If we have any grasp on God's mercy to us, we will be generous with our time and money in the service of others.
    2. The dynamic is seen in II Corinthians 8:2-3, where Paul tells us that the Macedonian Christians gave to the poor in Jerusalem out of their "extreme poverty." Such language indicates that the Macedonians were not any better off economically than the needy in Jerusalem. Their motivation could not possibly have been guilt over their own abundance. The dynamic for their mercy ministry was that they "knew" the grace of Christ who impoverished himself for our salvation.
        a. Christ did not say, "My blood is my own! Why should I give it away!" Therefore, we should not hold on to our money as if it were our own.
        b. Christ did not say, "These sinners are undeserving of my blood!" Neither should we withold mercy from the needy because we don't think they are "worthy" of it.
        c. Christ did not say, "Men might abuse my salvation." Christ knew that many people would reject his blood and even use it as an excuse for sinning more. Yet he came. Neither should we refuse to do mercy because we are afraid someone will misuse our aid.
    3. Because diaconal service is the natural response to grace, God can actually judge true from false Christians on judgment day by looking for deeds of mercy to the needy (Matt. 25:34ff.; Jas. 2:12-14). Any one who has no compassion for the helpless has not known the gospel of grace.
C. This motivation to mercy, then, exists in the heart of every true Christian. However, it is faint and weak in most of us. It must be nurtured.
    1. Paul prays for the Ephesians that they might know the

riches of their inheritance and the love of God (Eph. 1:18; 3:19). These believers already had a factual knowledge of these things. Rather, Paul sought that "the eyes of their hearts" would be enlightened. This refers to a growing penetration of the truth so that it dazzles the mind, inflames the emotions and fortifies the will. The Macedonian Christians "knew" the grace of Jesus Christ (II Cor. 8:9). The grace of Christ did not merely interest them. It thrilled, melted, and strengthened their hearts. They were impelled to do deeds of mercy.

2. As the truth of God's grace is comprehended, so the strength of our drive to do mercy is deepened. Only a growing motivation for mercy, arising out of a spreading doctrinal and spiritual understanding of God's grace will be a sufficient mainspring for service. Without this, diaconal workers will become too discouraged, weary, and cynical to follow Christ in his concern for the poor.

DISCUSSION QUESTIONS:

1. "The activity of 'deaconing' includes both an action and an attitude." Explain that statement. How prevalent is the deacon attitude in your congregation?

2. What specific things could you do in your church to foster the growth of the dynamic of mercy ministry?

Two Common Objections to the Ministry of Mercy

I. **The Church Does Not Really Have The Time or Money to Provide for the Needy!**
   ANSWER:
   A. First, we must ask: Does God require the church to provide for the needy?
      1. James 2:1-23 says true faith will always be characterized by good works, but the 'works' he speaks of is 'mercy' (see v. 13). Caring for the widow and the orphans (1:27), the poor man (2:6) and the hungry (2:15-16) are the examples used. Thus James says what Jesus says elsewhere (Matt. 25:31ff.). Namely, that a sensitive social conscience and a life poured out in deeds of mercy to the needy is an essential mark of true faith. God can gauge faith by deeds of mercy (cf. Matt. 25:45 with James 2:13).
      2. Matthew 11:1-6 tells us John the Baptist sought to know whether Jesus was really the Messiah. Christ offered evidence that he healed the sick and preached to the poor! Both the ministry of mercy and the ministry of the word was in the Kingdom agenda of Jesus.
      3. Acts 6:1-6 shows us that 'mercy' is not only the work of individual Christians, but also the church. Deacons are established as a permanent office in the church to carry on aid to the needy.
   B. Now we can ask, does the church have the time or the money to do mercy? The answer is clear. The church is commanded to evangelize the world, build up the saints, and aid the needy. We do not have the money or the resources to completely accomplish any of these tasks. But we must use what we do have to do all that God commands us to do. To fail to provide anything God orders us to do is sin.

II. **Most Poor People in America Are Simply Unwilling to Work**
   ANSWER: Biblically there are three causes of poverty.
   A. "Oppression." The Hebrew word most often translated "the poor" in the Old Testament means "wrongfully dispossessed." Oppression is any social condition or unfair treatment that brings or keeps a person in poverty (Ps. 82:1-8; 72:4; Prov. 14:31; Ex. 22:21-27). The Bible mentions unjustly low wages (Deut. 24:15), political/court systems weighted toward the rich and powerful (Lev. 17:15), and high interest loans (Ex. 22:25-27) as examples.
   B. "Disaster." Natural calamity, crop failure, financial misjudgment, disease or injury are just a few factors in this category.

There is no moral blame attached to this condition. An honest poor man has nothing to be ashamed of (Prov. 19:1, 22; cf. Lev. 25:39-43 'waxing poor').

C. "Sin." The third cause the Bible recognizes is sin. Laziness (Prov. 6:6-11), luxury-seeking (21:17), problems of self-discipline (23:21) can result in poverty.

It is fair to notice that outside of Proverbs, the "lazy poor" is mentioned very little. The majority of references of poverty in the Bible are not negative or scornful. It is therefore simplistic to pre-judge poor people as lazy, just as it would be to think they are all righteous. In reality, in almost all cases, all three root causes are present and inter-related.

DISCUSSION QUESTIONS:

1. Does this study challenge your thinking? Where?

    Does this study change your thinking? Where?

2. Why is it important to distinguish between causes of poverty?

Five Common Questions on Evaluating Need

I. **Shouldn't the Church Help Only Needy Christians?**
   A. On the one hand, we are told to help all people in need. The point of the parable of the Good Samaritan (Luke 10:25ff) is that we are to give mercy to anyone who we find in our path, even our enemies!
   B. On the other hand, we are told to give aid "especially to the household of faith" (Gal. 6:10). We are to give Christians the priority in our help.

II. **How Poor Must a Person be Before the Church Helps Him?**
   A. Poverty can be defined as a limitation of choices. The richer you are, the more choices you have as to travel, eating, leisure activity, clothes you wear, and so on. Wealth and poverty is a relative matter. Every individual knows persons with more economic options (who are "richer") and with fewer (who are "poorer").
   B. Luke 3:11 tells us if we have two coats, we should give to him with no coats so we both have one. In II Corinthians 8:13-14 Paul says the richer church should give to the poorer "that there may be equality."
   C. This does not mean we must force a kind of "economic leveling" on all church members. It means that when a person expresses a need, if he is "poorer" than you, he is a proper object of your diaconal concern! We do not help people only when they are destitute. Anyone with less choices than you should be aided (cf. Lev. 19:18. Do we wait until we are "in the gutter" to help ourselves? Neither should we wait until our brother is!)
   D. In a middle class church, look for members who are elderly, single-parent families, families with chronic illnesses, and the unemployed. There will be plenty of needs there.

III. **Should We Give Aid to People Who Brought Their Poverty On Themselves (by their own sin or laziness)?**
   A. The basic answer to this question is: "Yes, we should aid them." Romans 5:7-10 reminds us Christ did not only give his mercy to those whose misery was not their fault! He died while we were enemies. If we offer spiritual help to those whose trouble stems from sin, why not offer economic help to the same? From God's perspective, all of us have done deeds worthy of (not just poverty but) hell!
   B. Yet mercy must limit itself if a person continually uses our aid to further his irresponsible behaviour. I Timothy 5:8-14 tells us widows who were idlers or gossips were not to receive regular aid.

If a person rejects financial counseling or other counseling, the church may have to withdraw aid, but *always for the needy person's own good.* Only mercy can limit mercy.

IV. **Should We Help Strangers and Travelers, Persons Whose Sincerity We Cannot Judge?**
   A. Yes, we should give to strangers and sojourners (Heb. 13:2). Nabal refused David aid because he was a stranger, but this act is not seen in a favorable light (I Sam. 25).
   B. We are likely to be sometimes "ripped off" by travelers, but we are to be kind to the ungrateful and the selfish and to those who borrow without repaying (Luke 6:27-36).
   C. Nevertheless, we are not to make it easy for people to sin against us. We need to learn how to aid travelers without using cash, how to check with local welfare agencies and police departments, etc.

V. **Should We Only Aid Those Who Ask for Economic Help, or Should We Offer It?**
   ANSWER: Jesus did not wait for us to ask for his mercy! "You have not chosen me, I have chosen you," he said. He offers it — so should we!
   DISCUSSION QUESTION:
   Using the criteria listed on this sheet, make a list of persons inside the congregation and outside the congregation who need your aid.

The Three "Levels" of Mercy

Introduction:
The Bible teaches us that true religion is to help the needy in their affliction (Jas. 1:27). But how do we "help?" There are three levels of help for the poor which the Bible outlines.

I. **The First Level Is Simple Relief.**
We must first alleviate the immediate need so as to relieve the person's misery. The service of the Good Samaritan to the victim in the road was relief. The Samaritan met the man's immediate needs for medical care, for physical protection, for transportation, and for the financing of the convalescence. The work of relief has two aspects.
   A. We should seek out and involve ourselves in the lives of the needy. Jesus became poor (Luke 1:48, II Cor. 8:9), touched lepers (Mark 1:40-42), and socialized with outcasts (Luke 7:34).
   B. We should give not just "spot relief" but whatever is necessary to eliminate the need. We must give until his need is gone (Deut. 15:8, 10; II Cor. 8:13-14; Luke 3:11).

II. **The Second Level Is Economic Development.**
In Psalm 41:1, the man is pronounced "blessed" who "considers" the poor. The latter word means careful thinking toward a practical program of action. God is not interested in merely relief, but in the restoration of the poor to economic self-sufficiency. When a slave was released from his debts and servitude, his former master was to furnish him with animals from his flock, grain, and seeds, so that he has the "capital" to begin his own business (Deut. 15:13-14, "When thou sendest him out free from thee, thou shalt not let him go away empty; Thou shalt furnish him *liberally* out of thy flock, and out of thy floor, and out of thy wine press of that wherewith the Lord thy God has blessed thee, thou shalt give unto him"). Here is a clear command to the farmer to help set up his former slave in farming, too.

John Perkins writes that simply putting welfare checks in the hands of poor blacks only ends up transferring mere capital into the accounts of the wealthy white bankers and store owners in their town. Government poverty programs provided "relief," but did not work for community ownership, so blacks stayed dependent and poor. When Perkins in rural Mississippi communities began organizing the poor into farming co-ops, housing co-ops, and even banking co-ops, they were able to keep money and jobs in their neighborhoods. Not hand-outs but ownership is the way to break the cycle of poverty.[1]

III. **The Third Level of Mercy Is Social Reform (or social action).**
Social reform moves beyond relieving physical needs and seeks to change the social conditions and structures that create those needs. It does not just "patch up" the wounded but it goes after those who have

done the wounding. Job tells us that he not only clothed the naked, but he "broke the fangs of the wicked oppresser, and made him drop his victim" (Job 29:15-16).

The prophets of the Old Testament made many ringing calls for social reform. Unfair wages (Jer. 22:13), corrupt business practices (Amos 8:2,6), legal systems weighted in favor of the rich and powerful (Deut. 24:17; Lev. 19:15), a system of unfairly high interest loans (Lev. 19:35-37; 25:37; Ex. 22:25-37) were all denounced and opposed by the prophets. And not only did this kind of reform movement go on within the covenant community, but in exile Daniel calls the pagan government into account for its lack of mercy to the poor (Dan. 4:27).

The jubilee law, (Lev. 25 — which redistributed the land every 50 years to those families who had lost their original holdings), and the sabbath year law, (Deut. 15 — which forgave all debts every seventh year) are examples of social structures legislated by God to protect the poor.

Historically, Christians in times of revival have sought changes in social structure in the interest of justice and mercy. The fruit of the Great Awakening in 18th century England was the abolition of slavery, the reform of child labor laws, prison conditions and poor housing conditions among factory laborers.

Theologians disagree regarding how Christians should institute social reforms. What reforms should be instituted through the local church, and what reforms should be instituted through voluntary organizations of Christians? Should the session of a church endorse a political candidate? Should a presbytery or general assembly lobby for congressional legislation? What are the limits of such activities?

One thing is certain. Christians, through various channels, are required by God to work for a society that protects the poor and needy.

Footnote: [1]John Perkins, **A Quiet Revolution.**

DISCUSSION QUESTIONS:

1. What could your church be doing in the area of economic development?
2. Do you believe the church **as** church should work for social reform?
3. What are you doing personally to work for "justice in the gate" (in your government and society)?

ACTION PLAN

1. What are the most important things which you have learned from this article? List them.

2. Select two or three things which you would like to see put into practice in your church? Name them.

3. In order to implement these, do you need:
   ____ More or better information (about a program, your church, your community, etc.)? What is it?
   ____ More or better skills (abilities, expertise, etc.)? What are they?
   ____ More or better support from key people? Who are they?
   ____ More or better resources (such as money, facilities, personnel, etc.)? What are they?

4. Make a brief plan for securing each of the elements you lack. How could you get information, develop skills, win people's support, raise funds, and so on?

RESOURCES FOR DEACONS

Organizing For Diaconal Ministry

The Biblical Office of Deacon

I. **The Nature of the Office**
   A. **Its origin.** Acts 6:1-6. Deacons were given the ministry of distribution to the needy, the ministry of mercy, while the elders kept the ministry of "the word" (v. 4). The office of deacon is a permanent office in the church (I Tim. 3).
   B. **Its history.** In the early church, deacons actively visited in their communities, looking for the sick, the poor, the widows and orphans to whom they could give comfort and aid. In the middle ages the office of deacon evolved into merely assistants to the priest in the performance of the worship ritual. John Calvin alone of the Reformers re-established the diaconate with its biblical ministry of help to the poor and needy. However, deacons in Reformed churches during the past century are beginning to again lose sight of their reason for existance. They are evolving into merely treasurers and janitors. The ministry of mercy to the physical/economic needs of people is slowly being squeezed out of deacons, budgets and schedules.
   C. **Its purpose.** The office of deacon is designed to meet the *physical* needs of people. However, this ministry is a spiritual ministry, since it arises from spiritual motives (the experience of God's grace, Luke 6:33-36) and makes a spiritual impact (Acts 4:33, Phil. 4:10-20).

II. **The Qualifications for the Office**
   A. **Character.** I Timothy 3:8-13 tells us deacons must be: 1) "grave" — realistic and practical, 2) "not double-tongued" — honest, 3) "not greedy" — simple in their lifestyle, 4) "holding to the faith

with clear conscience" — practicing what they preach, 5) "not given to much wine" — self-controlled, 6) "managing his family well" — a good leader of his family, 7) "proved" — experienced in the faith. Deacons had better not be phonies nor easily discouraged! The people they will work with can spot phonies and can try patience.

B. **Gifts.** Romans 12:8 and I Corinthians 12:28 tell us of spiritual gifts of "deaconing" (service), "giving," "helps," and "administrations" that deacons can have.

III. The Work of the Diaconate

A. **Mercy.** To meet physical/economic needs inside and outside of the congregation. Visiting the sick, the poor, the elderly, single parent families and helping families in emergencies are included under this heading.

B. **Stewardship.** To encourage and promote liberal giving by the congregation, and then to collect and distribute those financial gifts. Stewardship education, envelope systems, counting, recording, depositing and reporting funds are included under this heading.

C. **Property.** To keep all the properties of the congregation in good repair and maintenance, and to control their use.

D. **Helps.** To accomplish the practical tasks and errands that are entailed in the on-going program of the church. Ushering, setting up equipment and chairs are included in this category.

Although these duties are not necessarily performed by the deacons, the deacons are responsible for their discharge.

IV. The Relationships of the Diaconate

The deacons have as much authority as the elders delegate to them. The elders are required by Scripture and Presbyterian polity to delegate to the deacons at some level of authority the work of mercy and stewardship. Deacons are not a separate legislative body (as the House of Representatives is to the Senate, for instance). Though the elders may overrule the deacons on any matter, a wise and godly session will seldom overturn deacons' decisions. Elders are not to rule in a domineering way, always "pulling rank" (I Peter 5:3). The session should routinely review all diaconal decisions and work.

V. The Preparation for the Diaconate

The process of education and training for deacons must be continuous.

A. Study the doctrinal and polity standards of your denomination.

B. Study the personal characteristics of a deacon and leader: Gene Getz, **The Measure of a Man,** Regal, Glenside, Calif.

C. Study the general duties of a deacon: Andrew Jumper, **Chosen to**

Serve, John Knox Press, Atlanta, Ga; G. Berghoef and L. Dekoster, **The Deacons Handbook,** Christian's Library Press, Grand Rapids, Mich.
D. Study the biblical basis for the ministry of mercy: G. Berghoef and L. DeKoster, **God's Yardstick,** Christian's Library Press; Harvey Conn, **Bible Studies on World Evangelization and Simple Lifestyle.**
E. Study a concrete example of a healthy mercy ministry: John Perkins, **A Quiet Revolution,** Word, Waco, Texas.

DISCUSSION QUESTIONS:
1. Do the elders of your church use the deacons effectively?
2. How could the session give the diaconate more help and/or freedom to do its ministry?

Two Proposals for Committees of the Diaconate

For most diaconates to be effective, deacons must specialize. Not only should there be specialization from committee to committee, but members of each committee could have distinct areas of ministry for which they are responsible. Below is a suggested list for four possible diaconal committees.

Some churches would be able to staff these committees entirely with deacons. But even in these churches, each committee should appoint a circle of laypersons to assist them with their tasks. In smaller churches, one or two deacons may head up a committee of 5-10 people.

In nearly every case, a board of deacons should have at least one committee — the mercy committee. Unless some deacons are told to work primarily on mercy, the work will be constantly usurped in the deacons' schedule by more urgent (but perhaps less important) responsibilities.

I. **Finance Committee (or stewardship committee)**
   A. Budget preparation.
   B. Budget control and disbursements.
   C. Counting and depositing financial gifts.
   D. Providing envelopes for gifts and recording contributions.
   E. Reports on receipts and disbursements to the congregation.
   F. Stewardship promotion and education.

II. **Property Committee**
   A. Supervision of sexton and anyone hired for maintenance of building and grounds.
   B. Maintenance and repair of church building, grounds, manse, and other property.
   C. Oversight of the use of all property and equipment of the congregation.
   D. Purchase of new items of property and equipment as they are needed (major purchases are to be recommended to the congregation).

III. **Helps Committee**
   A. Ushering and collections at services.
   B. Lighting, opening and locking, and ventilation of the rooms and buildings used for services and programs.
   C. Monitoring the taping of sermons and PA systems during service.
   D. Counting and keeping attendance records.

IV. **Mercy Committee**
   A. Care for the sick and shut-in.
   B. Care for the elderly.
   C. Care for the institutionalized (prisons, nursing homes, rehabilitation hospitals).
   D. Care for the handicapped and disabled.
   E. Care for single parent families.
   F. Meeting emergency needs for food, shelter, funds.
   G. Helping the economically needy by job counseling, financial counseling.
   H. Promotion of giving to the distant poor.
   I. Promotion of church involvement in national and regional disaster response.

   (Note: Members of the mercy committee should specialize. For example, one member could become an "expert" on finding jobs and vocational counseling for the unemployed. One member could be an "expert" on housing by knowing or arranging for various emergency shelters, low-cost temporary housing, and so forth. Another member could head up ministries to the sick, elderly, and handicapped. The deacons on the mercy committee could supervise actual access to the deacons' fund.)

DISCUSSION QUESTIONS:
   1. How is your board of deacons organized? Even if there is not a formal structure, is there an unwritten division of labor?
   2. Are all four areas of responsibility being covered?
   3. How could you better organize your board?

Many congregations have developed a network of smaller fellowship groups, usually organized geographically, in which worship, Bible study, and fellowship takes place. These are called "shepherding groups," "house churches" and many other names.

In churches with such a network, the following deacon board structure may be useful.

A. General Deacons.
   1. Make collections and disbursements to the deacons' fund and to all other funds.
   2. Oversee all mercy ministries of the congregation.
   3. General deacons will often meet separately from other deacons to review requests for diaconal aid and the mercy work of the church.

B. House Church Deacons.
1. Each house church shall have at least one house church deacon.
2. House church deacons communicate mercy needs within their house churches to the deacons' board.
3. House church deacons have referred to them mercy needs of families in their geographical area. The house church deacon mobilizes the resources of the house church to meet the need.
4. The house church deacons sit on the board with general deacons and share responsibilities for property and helps with them.

C. Ministry Deacons.
1. Ministry deacons are ordained to specific mercy ministries, such as a prison ministry or the operation of a halfway house, and so on.
2. Such ministries should be seen as "full-time" and therefore, ministry deacons should not be given other duties in areas such as property and helps.

Evaluation of Present Diaconal Ministry

The following is a worksheet which should be used in a large group discussion with the entire board of deacons. Have members brainstorm to list as many needs and problems as they see in each of the six areas. When the "Need/Problem" column is full, go back and isolate one or two of the greatest needs in each area. Finally, discuss solutions to each specific need and list them in the "Solution/Steps to take" column. Do all of this on a blackboard or an overhead projector, not on the sheet of paper below.

AREA	NEED/PROBLEM	SOLUTION/STEPS TO TAKE
1. Deacon motivation		
2. Deacons' skills		
3. Recruitment/ supervision of volunteers		
4. Board structure		
5. Resources/ inventories available (money, equipment, etc.)		
6. Support of staff and congregation		

The following questions will help a diaconate better evaluate its actual mercy ministry.

1. What duties do your deacons actually perform? Number each type of work below in terms of the priority given it in time and energy by your board. ('1' would be the highest priority and '5' the lowest). Also, estimate the percentage of the board's time devoted to each.

	Priority	% time
Helping the sick, aged, poor		
Collecting and disbursing monies		
Property maintenance		
Ushering; helps		
Other _____		

2. Do you have a deacons' fund or budget item for people with physical/economic needs?
If yes, what percentage of the total budget of the church is it? Does that seem like a fair and just proportion?

3. How many individuals or families in your congregation received **direct assistance** (financial or practical help) in the past year? How many families in the outside community received direct assistance in the past year?
4. How many individuals or families in your congregation have received **diaconal support** (help in finding jobs, counseling in financial matters, caring and listening, etc.) in the past year? How many families in the outside community received diaconal support from your church?
5. How effective has your direct assistance and support been? Were you able to give aid in a way that did not foster dependency? Was there evidence of growing economic self-sufficiency in the families with which you worked?

Diaconal Spiritual Gifts

Deacons should have spiritual gifts which relate closely to the ministry of mercy. They must also be able to identify and use such gifts in the congregation. The gifts of service, helps, giving, mercy, and hospitality exist in large numbers throughout the body of Christ, but they are not valued or utilized. Most positions in churches are teachers, leaders, administrators, and governors. But Christians with mercy gifts, though attracting little attention, are probably more numerous. Church leaders must become adept at discovering and finding positions for persons with these gifts. An outline of these gifts follows.

I. **Giving (Rom. 12:8)**

   A. Definition: The ability to contribute one's material resources with great generosity and cheerfulness, and to do so in such a way that bears spiritual fruit.

   B. Bible passages. II Corinthians 8:2, 3; 9:7-12; Philippians 4:16-19.

   C. Uses of the gift. 1) Gifted givers can be deacons who inspire liberality in the people by their example. 2) Gifted givers should form a network of people within the congregation who are contacted by deacons when emergencies arise.

   D. Discovering this gift. 1) Do you get a great deal of joy and satisfaction from giving? 2) Are you easily and profoundly moved by economic needs when you see them? 3) Do you gladly lower your standard of living to give? 4) Do you seldom if ever worry about your own financial stability and needs? 5) Are you good at managing money? (A gifted giver should answer "yes" to these questions.)

II. **Service (Rom. 12:7)**

   A. Definition: The ability to see and meet temporal needs, especially in such areas that are involved in tasks related to God's work.

   B. Bible passages. Luke 22:24-27; II Timothy 1:16-18; Matthew 25:34-36.

   C. Uses. Persons with practical skills should be placed in a "talent bank" which keeps track of the congregation's abilities in order to mobilize them to meet physical/economic needs in the body. Persons with service gifts should schedule time each week for diaconal ministry.

   D. Discovering this gift. 1) Do you enjoy working with your hands? 2) Are you seldom annoyed when called upon to do odd jobs and repairs around the house, though others get bored with them? 3) Are you able to spot practical needs? 4) Do you get impatient with planning and theorizing and prefer to get down to practical doing?

III. Mercy (Rom. 12:8)
   A. Definition: The ability to feel love and sympathy for people who are suffering and to alleviate the suffering through kind deeds.
   B. Bible passages. Luke 17:11-14; Luke 10:29-37; Matthew 20:30-34; Mark 10:46-52; I Thessalonians 5:14.
   C. Uses. Medical professionals should have the gift of mercy. The gift also equips people to do volunteer work in hospitals, nursing homes, prisons, homes for the handicapped, etc.
   D. Discovering this gift. 1) Do you find your heart goes out to people in pain? 2) Do you find you can be patient and affectionate to people to whom no one else can be? 3) Do you get satisfaction out of visiting the sick and the elderly?

IV. Helps (I Cor. 12:28)
   A. Definition: The ability to invest time and talents in assisting people to "free them up" for their own ministries.
   B. Bible passages. Romans 16:1, 2; Acts 20:34-35; Numbers 11:16-17; Luke 8:1-3; Genesis 2:20-23.
   C. Uses. The gift of "helps" equips people to be administrative assistants, teachers or nurses aides, secretaries, pastor's helpers, etc.
   D. Discovering this gift. 1) Do you prefer to be an assistant to a leader rather than a leader? 2) Do you prefer to do "behind the scenes" work and do you avoid recognition and acclaim? 3) Do you enjoy doing "menial" tasks to free up other Christians to do their jobs?

Reading: C. Peter Wagner, **Your Spiritual Gifts Can Help Your Church Grow.** (Glendale: Regal, 1978)

DISCUSSION QUESTION:

How could your church keep an "inventory" of your church's diaconal gifts?

Diaconal Ministry and Church Growth

I. **The Problems**
Church leaders often perceive a tension between service or diaconal ministries and growth or evangelistic ministries.
   A. The Resource Problem.
      1. Diaconal ministries are expensive. Limited financial resources are stretched thin to support both mercy and evangelistic ministries.
      2. Diaconal ministries are time consuming. Pastors and lay leaders are often not equipped with the management skills necessary to begin them. In many cases, evangelistic ministries suffer when leaders' time is consumed by a diaconal ministry.
   B. The Priority Problem.
   It is very difficult to keep growth ministries and service ministries in perfect balance. Each one tends to absorb the time needed for the other. Which then should be given *priority?*

II. **Theological Guidelines**
   A. The church is to do the work of the kingdom.
      1. The kingdom of God is the renewal of the whole world through the introduction of supernatural forces. God is working to destroy all the disordering effects of sin on the world (see Gen. 3:17ff.) by uniting all things under his rule in Christ. In Ephesians 1:9-10 we are told that God has an economy (an "**oikonomia**" — a blueprint of a house) for the universe. He wants to make the whole world his home again. Then all hurts will be healed.
      2. The church is to be both a model for his kingdom (we are God's household — Gal. 6:10) and an agent for the spread of his kingdom (Acts 8:12; 19:8; 20:25).
   B. The work of the kingdom includes both service ministries and growth ministries.
      1. In John 17:18 Jesus sends the apostles and therefore the church into the world as he was sent into the world. Jesus did both the ministry of the word and deeds of mercy in the world (Luke 24:19; Matt. 11:5-6). The mission of the church includes both evangelism and deeds of mercy.
      2. In Matthew 5:43-48 and Luke 6:27-36 we are told that our deeds of mercy should extend to all men even as God makes the rain to fall on the just and the unjust. Our diaconal ministry should reflect God's common grace as well as his special grace.

C. Strictly speaking, mercy and evangelism are equally necessary because they are both commanded by God. There is no theological priority to be given to one over the other. However, as stated above, one or the other will have to be given some actual priority in time and money. The "context" of a church — its needs, problems and opportunities along with those of the society around it will determine actual priority of growth ministries and service ministries.
  1. When there is a natural disaster (such as a flood or famine), diaconal ministry may need to have priority in the use of a church's resources. When there is rampant oppression and injustice in a society, it may be necessary for a church to witness for the kingdom by taking a stand on a social issue which will bring it persecution and a loss of members. In such contexts, diaconal aid comes first.
  2. However, though growth ministries and service ministries are equally required by God, evangelism is a more basic and radical ministry to the human condition. This is true not because the spiritual is more important than the physical. (God created both and he will redeem both.) Rather, the eternal is more important than the temporal (II Cor. 4:16-18). Aid given to our bodies is aid given to a temporary entity. Therefore, ordinarily, evangelistic ministries will have an actual if slight priority in the overall ministry of the church obedient to the word of God.

III. The Evangelistic Impact of Diaconal Ministry
A. Diaconal ministry creates a positive image in the outside community.
  1. In Luke 6:32, Jesus tells us that there is nothing remarkable about a particular group taking care of its own poor and needy. However, when Christians take care of the needy of the world, they are unique.
  2. Therefore, our good deeds glorify God before men (Matt. 5:16). An early opponent of Christianity complained, "Nothing has contributed to the supersitition of these Christians more than their charity to strangers . . . the impious Galileans provide not only for their own poor, but for ours as well."
B. Diaconal ministry creates a corporate witness to the love of Christ.
  1. Jesus taught that when Christians love one another in a visible way, the world will know that Christ has come (John 17:23).
  2. One of the most impressive and visible ways in which Christians demonstrate their love for one another is by

mutual diaconal ministry and economic sharing. When they "sold their possessions . . . and gave them to all men, as each had need" (Acts 2:45) then they had "favor with all the people" (Acts 2:47). When "they had all things in common" (Acts 4:32) then "with great power gave the apostles witness of the resurrection" (Acts 4:33).

C. Diaconal ministry builds bridges for growth ministries.
1. Diaconal ministries bring the church into contact with many non-Christians to whom the gospel can be shared.
2. Persons contacted through diaconal ministries will generally be more receptive to your church than people who you contact "cold" through visitation or advertising. You have already shown them compassion.
3. Often, persons who have been helped by a service ministry and who come to Christ can be more easily assimilated into the life of the church. They already know a number of people in the church and may already be part of a church group.
4. Careful planning and persevering follow up is necessary to capitalize on the growth potential of diaconal ministry.
   a. Keep a careful record of everyone contacted and served by the diaconal program.
   b. Have a consistent, organized series of visits made to each contact. Be sure the gospel is presented in the course of those visits.
   c. Plan other "felt need" activities or programs to which your contacts can be invited.

DISCUSSION QUESTIONS:
1. Is your diaconate convinced that diaconal ministries are necessary for your church to be a witness to the kingdom? Is your congregation?
2. Have you any service ministries to the community (e.g. a blood bank, a Christian school, a crisis pregnancy center, a food bank or clothing closet, etc.)? Have you a detailed and careful plan for making the most of this ministry's growth potential? What should you do?

Steps for Mobilizing a Church for Mercy Ministry

Step I — Teaching
  A. Mercy is commanded by God, but it cannot be simply the response to a demand. It must arise from hearts made gracious by the experience of God's mercy. It is therefore improper to simply impose mercy ministry programs on the congregation "from the top." Instead, the congregation must be exposed to God's word concerning deed ministry and the dynamic of deed ministry, namely the doctrines of grace.
  B. Preaching and teaching must carefully and thoroughly lay the foundation for mercy ministry in a church. John the Baptist's sermon cut the listeners to the heart until they cried out "What shall we do then?" (Luke 3:10). It was then that John directed them to share food and clothing with the needy (v. 11).
  C. Some educational materials for the people include:
    1. John Stott. **Who is my Neighbor?** (Inter-Varsity)
    2. Harvie Conn. **Evangelism: Doing Justice and Preaching Grace** (Zondervan)
    3. John Perkins. **With Justice for All** (Regal)

Step II — Surveying
  A. Many churches who seek to aid the poor and needy are more reactive than active. That is, deacons respond to cries for help from individuals or from existing social relief organizations. But deacons should also be seeking out needs and discovering the opportunities for mercy ministry in their community. What groups of people in your area have the most critical unmet needs?
  B. To make these discoveries, conduct a survey of your community. See the article below entitled "Community Needs Assessment."

Step III — Making Contact
  A. Many churches begin clothing closets or other such ministries to the needy but find that no one takes advantage of the provision since no contact has been made with the people in need. How can deacons be sure to "spade up" enough mercy needs so that a vital ministry can be undertaken?
  B. Some methods:
    1. Community involvement. Encourage members to become involved in private or secular social service and helping organizations. Also, identify every member of your church who is already involved in such work. Use these members as bridges to the needy they know and work with.

2. Directly contact the local welfare or social services department and communicate your interest in helping with persons in need.
3. Do regular diaconal visitation in needy neighborhoods. Seek needs and offer help. Regular diaconal visitation in members' homes will also help deacons spot mercy needs.
4. Place a card or sheet of paper in the pew which provides a place for people to ask deacons for help or to inform deacons of mercy needs in the congregation or community. (See article on Service Bank on pages 50FF.)
5. Public listing. Place an advertisement and a phone number in a local paper offering mercy help to those who need it.

Step IV — Organizing the Leadership

A. Mercy is the work of the whole church (as is the work of evangelism, discipleship, and worship), but the leadership of the church must be organized to facilitate the congregation's ministry.

Methods:
1. Specialization. (See article on "Two Proposals for Committees of the Diaconate" on pages 32 and 33.)
2. Ministry teams. Deacons must be trained to investigate and evaluate economic needs in teams of two. Whenever a need is referred to the deacons, it is assigned to a ministry team. (For more on what a ministry team does, see all the articles in the last section of this notebook, under the heading "Casework in Diaconal Ministry.")
3. Mercy committee. (See article on "Two Proposals for Committees of the Diaconate".)

Step V — Organizing the Congregation

A. When needs arise, deacons must know where to go for the resources to meet them. All the church's resources of money, gifts, man-hours, food, homes, etc. must be gathered and organized to be used in an orderly way at the word of the deacons.

B. Methods:
1. The Deacon's Fund. (See page 48.)
2. The Service Bank. (See pages 50FF.)
3. Special networks. Enlist networks of families and individuals who agree to contribute money, provide hospitality, or give some other resource when a need arises.
4. Mission groups. (See page 54.)

Surveying Your Community for Diaconal Needs

Most church people believe they know the hurts and needs of the community in which they live. Experience proves that this is not the case. Most middle class Americans live in isolation from the needy. Many social needs are not visible to the casual observer. Therefore, a formal, well-planned survey of the community is necessary.

I. **Determine Procedures**
   A. Make appointments. Don't just "drop in" on resource people. You will get more information and help if the person is not impatient to end your interview and get back to his or her scheduled duties.
   B. Explain your goals briefly (see below).
   C. Always ask the person you are interviewing for a list of other resource people you should contact.
   D. Many of the persons you interview may ask for help from you or your church. There will be a tendency for you to respond positively to the first agencies you interview. As the survey proceeds, you will see that you cannot possibly meet all the needs. Beware of making any commitments, implied or otherwise, during your survey.

II. **Set Goals**
   A. Goal 1 — To discover the kinds, degrees, concentrations of and locations of human needs. In particular, you are searching out 1) the poor, 2) the elderly, 3) unwed mothers, 4) widowed and divorced single parents, 5) disadvantaged children, 6) juvenile offenders, 7) the physically and mentally disabled, 8) convicts and ex-convicts, 9) refugees.
   B. Goal 2 — To discover the existing public and private agencies that are carrying on programs which meet mercy needs in your community. Your goal is not only to learn of their existence, but also of their degree of effectiveness. An illustration of such a list of agencies is provided in the article, "The Ministry of Referral."
   C. Goal 3 — To discover the *gaps* between the needs of the community and the services provided. What needs are going unmet because there is no (or insufficient) action being taken to help?

III. **Contact Agencies**
   A. Local Welfare or Social Services Department.
      1. Ask: Are there any geographical areas where there is a high concentration of a particular need (e.g. an area where there are many refugees, poor elderly persons, etc.).
      2. Ask: How many people in this area receive assistance? Get

figures on: Medicaid, food stamps, Aid for Dependent Children (ADC), unemployment, Supplementary Security Income (SSI).
3. Ask: How many people are unemployed and whose benefits have run out (add this figure to the number of persons on unemployment).
4. Ask: What services or resources (beside the social services department) exist to give aid to the needy in the area?
   a. What private groups or voluntary organizations are there?
   b. Is there a community service directory available?
5. Ask: What are the needs which are the most neglected by existing services? What are the needs which the church could respond to with financial and personal aid?
6. Ask: Would your department be willing to refer needs to us and help us match our resources with the needs? Could you provide training for our volunteers?

B. Census Records and/or City (or County) Planner.
1. Look or ask for existing statistics:
   a. Income level by region.
   b. Occupation and educational level of heads of households by region.
   c. Size of families, size of house lots, real estate values by region.
   d. Number of single parent households; number of one person households.
   e. Breakdown of population by race, age, nationality/language; population characteristics by age and race and nationality.
2. Look or ask about the projected changes in population.
3. From these statistics much can be inferred, both about social needs and the location of concentrated needs.

C. Department of Health and Hospital Social Worker(s).
1. What are the prevalent needs and in what geographical areas? Ask for figures on home bound elderly, disabled, infant care, nutrition problems, and other chronic health problems.
2. What other private agencies and voluntary organizations are meeting health care needs? Is a directory available?
3. Ask again:
   a. What are the health care needs which are most neglected by existing services?

b. What are the needs which our church could meet with financial and personal aid?
c. Would your agency refer needs to us and help us match our resources with needy people?
d. Would you be willing to train our volunteers?

D. Department of Mental Health.
1. Ask for figures on mentally retarded, mentally ill, and any other categories the department keep track of. Ask about the living conditions of each category. How many are in: a) institutions, b) homes with family, c) independent housing, d) specialized housing?
2. What other private agencies or voluntary organizations exist to meet mental health needs? Is a directory of such organizations available?
3. Ask:
   a. What mental health needs are most neglected by existing services?
   b. What needs could our church meet?
   c. Would your agency be willing to refer needs to us and help us match our resources with needy people?
   d. Would you be willing to train our volunteers?

E. Public School Officials.
1. Ask for figures and location of the following needs:
   a. Single parent homes.
   b. Truancy and delinquency.
   c. Families who cannot nurture children.
   d. Drug and alcohol abuse.
   e. Child abuse.
   f. Families not receiving adequate nutrition and health care.
   g. Teenage pregnancy.
   h. Children and youth who need tutoring.
2. Ask: Are there private agencies and voluntary organizations who are meeting these needs? Is there a directory of such organizations available?
3. Ask:
   a. Which needs are the most neglected by existing services?
   b. Which needs can our church meet?
   c. Would your agency be willing to refer needs to us or help us match our resources with needy persons?

            d.   Would you be willing to train our volunteers?
- F. Other Agencies:
    1. Go also to police departments, juvenile courts, veterans administration, other clergymen, job placement and vocational counseling offices, area realtors, and so on.
    2. Ask each of them:
        a. What are the needs?
        b. What are the existing services?
        c. What are the gaps between needs and services?

III. **Write a summary of your survey using the outline of the three goals: needs, services and gaps.**

Guidelines for a Deacon's Fund

Introduction

A Deacons' Fund is a sum of money set apart to help people in need. *Any* church, regardless of size or financial situation, can establish such a fund. The following outline is a hypothetical set of by-laws for the operation of such a deacons' fund. Any deacons seeking to use the outline will need to modify it for their own situation.

I. **Purpose**
  A. The name of the fund shall be called "the Deacons' Fund."
  B. This fund will be used exclusively to aid people who have financial and physical needs, and who (therefore) need both the spiritual and economic help of the church.

II. **Compilation of Funds**
  A. This fund will receive money budgeted yearly from the operating budget of the church. Ordinarily, the Deacons' Fund will be no less than three percent of the total budget of the church.
  B. This fund will be supplemental by special offerings at services set by the deacons with the approval of the session.
  C. Designated gifts to the Deacons' Fund will be received.

III. **Access to Funds**
  A. A treasurer will keep at all times $200.00 in cash in his home for emergencies.
  B. Any two deacons who agree on a need may spend up to $75.00 in an emergency without the consent of the entire diaconate. Larger sums must be approved by a majority of the board.
  C. Two deacons shall at all times have the power to sign checks from the Deacons' Fund.

IV. **Priorities**
  A. Setting an order of priority on needs:
    1. Does **not** mean funds should be withheld from a "lower" priority group until it is seen whether "higher" priority groups have needs that year.
    2. **Does** mean that expenditures to higher priority groups shall usually be larger and more extensive. When limited resources clearly require the deacons to choose between needs, the higher priority need will be met.
  B. The order of priority:
    1. The church members (Gal. 6:10) within this body:
      a. Retired members (the elderly).

            b. Single-parent families.
            c. Sick and handicapped.
            d. Others.
        2. Christian non-member who attends our church.
        3. Other Christians.
        4. Non-Christian friends and relatives of church members.
        5. Non-Christians living in the neighborhood/community of the church.
        6. Other non-Christians.
V. **Distribution of Help**
    A. Two deacons shall investigate any need coming to the deacons.
    B. The two deacons, if they recommend giving aid, form a ministry team which draws up a ministry plan concluding:
        1. The form of the help (single cash gift, loan, monthly payment, etc.).
        2. The conditions for the help, if any.
        3. Other ministry needed.
    C. Help or money shall never be sent by mail, but shall always be delivered in person by deacons.
        1. The deacons shall always explain the motivation behind the help, that they give because Christ has given to them.
        2. If the person being helped is a non-Christian, it is required that the gospel be presented to them at some time during the period of ministry.

The Service Bank: By-Laws

I. **Definition**

The Service Bank is an effort to identify and mobilize the gifts and skills of a congregation to make them available in an organized way to these practical human needs.

II. **Workers**

A. Coordinator. He or she: 1) Trains workers, 2) Acquires equipment and supplies needed, 3) Promotes and advertises the bank, 4) Receives needs, chooses possible resources, assigns names to callers, 5) Receives caller's results and records them, 6) Thanks the person who renders the service.

B. Callers. They: 1) Call persons in the order which the coordinator has referred to them. When one person indicates willingness, the caller stops calling. 2) Make sure the service has been rendered by asking the resource person to call him back when finished. 3) Relay to the coordinator all calls they make and the responses.

III. **Gathering the Resources**

A. All church members who are willing shall fill out a form dispersed by the coordinator. This form shall include: 1) Name, address, and phone, 2) Specific services the person can render, including child care, tutoring, sewing, providing transportation, medical care, moving and hauling, carpentry, yardwork, legal counsel, hospitality, electrical work, auto repair, accounting/bookkeeping, phone calling, caring for the convalescing, housecleaning, etc., 3) Times of the day and week when the person is more often available.

B. These forms should be given to new members and updated every year.

C. The results of these forms shall be stored as follows:

1. A card file shall be kept marked **RESOURCES.** On each card shall be the name, address and phone number of each person filling out a form, filed alphabetically.

2. A card file shall be kept marked **SERVICES.** Each service listed on the bank form shall have a card on which the names of all persons indicating willingness to perform services are listed.

IV. **Gathering the Needs**

A. "Need cards" shall be placed in pews and be referred to by the minister weekly. A need card has spaces to indicate the kind of service needed as well as the name of the person who needs it. Need cards can be filled out for oneself or for someone else. They may be put in the offering plate or given to a deacon or pastor.

    B.   Needs may come to the notice of pastors, elders, deacons or anyone else in the church. Such people can call the coordinators to tell him/her of a need.

V. **Ordinary Operation**

    A.   Coordinator receives a need card. (If he gets a phone call he fills out a need card anyway.)

    B.   He decides what service is necessary to meet the need.

    C.   He looks in the **SERVICES** file and writes down, on the back of the need card, four or five persons who can be called on to do the task.

    D.   He then checks the **RESOURCE** card of each individual. If he sees recorded there that one of these persons has rendered service recently, he scratches that name off the need card. He then assigns an order to the remaining names.

    E.   He then gives the need card to a caller (or phones it to a caller).

    F.   The caller calls the names in order until someone agrees to do the task. He asks the resource person to call him when it is complete.

    G.   The caller follows up the worker until he is sure the job is done. Then he contacts the coordinator and tells him who was called and what the response was.

    H.   The coordinator records on the resource cards who has done what and on what date. He keeps used need cards in a third file.

    I.   The coordinator expresses appreciation to the worker.

VI. **Priorities**

Officers must set priorities. Retired members and needy families must receive the swiftest and most extensive help. Aid must be given only to those who truly lack the resources to meet their own needs themselves. (For example, a lawyer in the congregation should not contact the service bank to paint his garage.)

For further study: **Caring Ministry.** Churches Alive!
Box 3800, San Bernadino, CA 92413

"Service-Talent Bank" Survey

Your deacons are conducting a survey in order that we may strengthen our fellowship and increase our outreach.

All of us have something to offer. Please complete the following survey and return it to one of the deacons.

(Remember, you are not agreeing to perform these services at all times or in any circumstances. **You** will choose.)

A. GENERAL INFORMATION

NAME _____ PHONE _____

ADDRESS _____ LICENSED DRIVER? _____

_____ CAR AVAILABLE? _____

B. SPECIFIC SERVICES YOU ARE CAPABLE OF RENDERING

- ____ supervision and care of children in my home
- ____ tutoring
- ____ sewing
- ____ providing transportation
- ____ clerical work (typing, filing, mailing)
- ____ medical and nursing assistance
- ____ moving and hauling (but I have no truck)
- ____ carpentry
- ____ visitation
- ____ legal advice
- ____ sitting with the elderly
- ____ hospitality (overnight) number of beds ____
- ____ hospitality (meals)
- ____ prayer (holding specific prayer requests before God)

- ____ babysitting in another home
- ____ cooking (in my home to be taken out)
- ____ cooking (outside my home) and serving
- ____ financial advice/counseling
- ____ housecleaning
- ____ photography
- ____ writing
- ____ electrical work
- ____ car repair
- ____ art work
- ____ accounting/bookkeeping
- ____ phone calling
- ____ mailing (folding, stuffing, addressing, i.e. bulletins)
- ____ plumbing

___ painting   ___ hair cutting/dressing
___ masonry

C. **OTHER SKILLS YOU HAVE OR SERVICES YOU COULD RENDER FOR THE BENEFIT OF OTHERS:**

_____

_____

D. **DAY AND TIME THAT YOU ARE MORE LIKELY TO BE AVAILABLE TO RENDER SERVICE. YOU MAY CHECK MORE THAN ONE. (NOTE: THIS DOES NOT IN ANY WAY OBLIGATE YOU TO REMAIN FREE AT THESE TIMES.)**

Sunday ___	Thursday ___	Morning ___
Monday ___	Friday ___	Afternoon ___
Tuesday ___	Saturday ___	Evenings ___
Wednesday ___		

Common questions regarding the Service-Talent Bank:

1. **Must I stay available if I put down that I am free most evenings?** No. Go about your regular schedule. Only when you're ready, willing, and able will you be contacted. Only the deacon who calls you will know you've been contacted.

2. **Will I be overworked?** Every effort will be made to spread the duties around. A record will be kept of how often you've been contacted, in order to avoid overloading anyone.

3. **Won't some people be too proud to share their needs?** That's a serious possibility, but it's only their loss. It hurts no one else.

4. **Won't some people take advantage of others?** This is always a risk any generous person takes. But Christians should do this less often than people who have never experienced God's spirit or known God's word. The officers will use their discernment to decide if someone is abusing the bank by thoughtlessly imposing on his brethren.

5. **What if only a small number in the church make themselves available?** Of all the potential problems, this one will most quickly kill the talent bank. If it happens, it will be a very telling indicator of the congregation's spiritual life.

Outline for Mission Groups

I. **Definition**
A mission group is a small group of five to twelve people who band themselves together for two purposes:
   A. "Inreach." That is, members are seeking to build *one another* up into he fullness of the stature of Christ.
   B. "Outreach." That is, members are seeking to witness to the world through speaking the words of the gospel and doing deeds of mercy.

II. **Inreach**
The program of inreach consists of the following endeavors:
   A. Learning to know God. Members must come to a deeper awareness of God's person, a greater desire for his glory, a more profound love of his fellowship, and a more complete discernment of and surrender to his will.
   B. Learning to know ourselves. Members must come to a clearer understanding of their gifts, strengths, and weaknesses. They must learn to foster steady spiritual growth and change.
   C. Learning to know others. Members must learn to establish biblical relationships with others. They must experience the pain and comfort of loving one another, submitting to one another, forgiving one another, correcting one another.

III. **Outreach**
Each mission group chooses an outreach mission. They should look for specific human needs which are going unfilled, and move to meet them.
Examples of mission groups' outreaches at the Church of the Saviour in Washington, D.C. and in other churches:
   A. One mission group recruits and trains families to be foster parents for homeless. It has developed over 100 such homes.
   B. One mission group has established a retreat center on a local farm and runs retreats for groups in the church or those outside the church.
   C. One mission group leads a bi-weekly Bible study at a local prison.
   D. One mission group leads a Bible class for retarded teenage girls at a local home for girls.
   E. One mission group operates a recreation program for neighborhood children at a local playground.
   F. One group leads classes, outings and other programs for senior citizens. They regularly visit shut-ins and provide weekly transportation for those without care.

- G. One mission group does tutoring for children and adults in their community.
- H. One mission group runs a "thrift shop" for low-income families in a poor neighborhood.
- I. One mission group leads weekly after-school Bible clubs at the church as an outreach to the neighborhood.
- J. One mission group works to restore older buildings and rents them at reasonable prices to low-income people.

IV. **Requirements for Membership**
- A. The person should be a Christian and should be committed to the purposes of the group.
- B. The person, with other members of the group, should submit to clear, specific disciplines. Minimum disciplines are:
  1. Daily prayer and Bible meditation.
  2. Weekly time of Bible study.
  3. Weekly worship.
  4. Attendance of small group meetings.
  5. Giving a set proportion of one's means to the Lord's work.
- C. In addition, the group may set other disciplines that the member must be committed to.
- D. At small group meetings, each member is accountable to share:
  1. How the disciplines have helped you grow, as well as where you have failed to grow.
  2. What God has been teaching you through the Scriptures.
  3. The "highs" and "lows" of your week.

V. **Formation**
- A. An individual with a desire and burden for a particular ministry begins to gather other Christians who have the same burden. This person (or small group of persons) can share his/her burden and vision for mission through worship services or other classes. If there is *not* a response, the person may wait for a better time, or try to do something less ambitious in mission him/herself.
- B. If a group is formed, they must develop a clear program and strategy by:
  1. Researching the needs and current services and programs.
  2. Taking inventory of the group's own gifts and resources.
  3. Planning a working strategy.
- C. Mission groups last as long as there are sufficient members within the group that have the burden for the mission outreach.

The Ministry of Referral

If officers have become familiar with the complex network of social service and relief resources in its community, a church can become a valuable referral agency for those under its pastoral care.

Deacons must have a balanced approach to the ministry of referral. On the one hand, the church may have a greater spiritual impact on a needy family if it can provide some of its *own* members to meet mercy needs. Also, many secular social service agencies may provide unbiblical counsel and guidance along with its aid. On the other hand, the church should not deplete all its resources when there are funds and aid available in the county to supplement the church's ministry.

Deacon's should compile a referral list of agencies and authorities in the area. In metropolitan areas, the United Way will often have a master list. Local welfare departments may have such a directory. The phone book of course is essential reading. The list should include each agency's (or professional's) name, address, telephone number and other information (hours, policies, fees, etc.). Below is a list of the type of agencies to look for:

Aging Programs

    Nursing Homes
    Developmental Day-Care Centers for the Aged
    All subsidized housing for the retired
    Foster Grandparents Programs
    Social Workers for Elderly
    Service Corp of Retired Executives
    American Association of Retired Persons
    Retired Senior Volunteer Program
    Nutrition Centers for Senior Citizens
    Local Government "Office of Aging"

Children/Youth

    Learning Disabilities Council
    Children's Defense Fund
    Infant Nutrition Centers
    Child Abuse/Neglect Social Workers
    Day-Care and Nursery Schools
    Foster Homes
    Pre-School "Head Start" programs
    Child Development Centers
    Big Brother/Sister programs
    Juvenile court officers
    Adoption agencies
    Parents Anonymous
    School guidance counselors

Legal
- Legal Aid Services
- Lawyers
- Magistrates and other court officers
- Juvenile Detention Centers
- "Poverty Law" Hotlines or Numbers
- Juvenile Justice Office

Housing
- Local Redevelopment & Housing Authorities
- Rental Assistance Offices
- County/City Offices on Housing
- State and Federal Housing Administration
- Numerous Emergency Shelters
- Federally subsidized housing complexes
- Building Inspectors

General Assistance
- Local Welfare Department Eligibility worker —
  - Aid for Dependent Children
  - Supplemental Security Income
  - Medicaid
  - "Social Security" (DASDHI)
  - Food Stamps
  - Fuel Assistance
  - School Lunch
- Traveler's Aid
- Salvation Army

Handicapped Services
- Rehabilitation Centers
- Developmental Activity Centers
- Mental Retardation Services Board
- Living/Training facilities for the Retarded
- Speech Centers
- Numerous Special Interest Organizations:
  - Epilepsy Association
  - Deaf Programs (TTY)
  - Larynjections
  - Lupus Foundation
  - Cerebral Palsy
  - Visually Handicapped

Health
- Emergency Crews
- Cancer Society
- Heart Association
- Public Health Clinics
- Public Health Nurses
- Doctor
- Hospitals
- Health Care Social Workers
- Lung Association
- Weight Watchers
- Medical Centers for Women
- Public Health Information Hotlines & Programs
- Crisis Pregnancy Centers

Consumer Information
- Better Business Bureau
- Consumer Credit Counseling Service
- Fair Housing Commission
- Equal Employment Opportunity Commission
- Consumer Protection Centers and Hotlines
- Food and Drug Administration

Education
- Literacy programs
- Tutorial programs
- Graduate Equivalence Degree Programs
- College/Vocational Schools
- Educational Grant Information Numbers

Employment/Vocational
- U.S. Employment Commissions
- Job Corps
- Occupational Work Centers

Other
- Urban League
- Rescue Missions
- Volunteers of America
- Veterans Administration

DISCUSSION QUESTION:

Let one deacon "specialize" in knowing the local resources for one or two of the ten categories of services listed above. Whenever a mercy need arises, it can be referred to a deacon "specialist."

Mercy Ministry Planning Worksheet

1. Name of the program _____
2. Description of the "target group" and needs to be met:

   _____
   _____
   _____

3. Description of the basic program strategy (method) to meet the needs:

   _____
   _____
   _____
   _____

4. Resources needed:
   a. Manpower
      1) How many people will be needed? _____
      2) What different positions and classes of workers will there be?

         _____
         _____

      3) What skills will be required for each job?

         _____
         _____

      4) How will they be recruited? _____

      5) What training will be required? _____

      6) Will a particular group in the church be responsible for the program? _____

   b. Facilities
      1) How much and what kind of space will be needed?

         _____
         _____

2) How often? _____
3) What other equipment or supplies will be needed?
_____

c. Finances
1) What will be the overall cost? _____
2) Will there be any income from the programs? _____
    How much? _____
3) What will be the estimated cost per year? _____
    per month? _____ per week? _____ per day? _____
4) What will be sources of income for the project?
_____

5) By what criteria will "success" be measured in this program?
_____

6) What specific steps will have to be taken to get from where we are to an operating status? (Assign a date-deadline to each step.)
a) _____ Date: _____
b) _____ Date: _____
c) _____ Date: _____
7) People responsible for the progress of this program according to plan: _____
_____

8) Any obstacles: _____

Presbytery Diaconal Associations

I. **Definition**

A diaconal association is an organization of deacons from the churches of a particular region united to carry out diaconal work in their region.

II. **Rationale**

Deacons should unite throughout the presbyteries and General Assembly to do their work because:

A. Paul marshalled the combined resources of the churches in Macedonia and Achaia to provide relief for the saints in Jerusalem (Romans 15:26). This is "connectional" diaconal work.

B. Presbyterianism recognizes that the "church" is larger than the local congregation. Paul teaches that no individual has all the gifts necessary for total ministry. As we promote connectional elder ministry, we should promote connectional diaconal ministry. This is consistent Presbyterianism.

C. The BCO (9-6) provides the basis for diaconal associations.

III. **Organization of a Presbytery Diaconal Association**

A. Purposes.

1. To establish fellowship between deacons.
2. To promote the work of deacons and to challenge them to the ministry of mercy.
3. To assist deacons in the meeting of needs in their churches and communities.
4. To coordinate the efforts and resources of churches and diaconates in meeting needs within the presbytery's area of ministry.

B. Steps to Establishment.

1. Form a Presbytery Diaconal Committee

    a. It shall be a standing committee of the presbytery.

    b. It shall consist of equal numbers of elders and deacons.

    c. To form it, the presbytery shall appoint the deacon members, and shall elect the elder members as with other standing committees.

    d. Duties:
    1) The PDC will serve as the executive committee of the Diaconal Association.
    2) The PDC will report routinely at each presbytery meeting.

3) The PDC will be given authority along with its association to raise and disburse funds for all activities necessary to carry out its purposes. Its budget will be separate from that of presbytery, but must be approved by presbytery.
4) The PDC and association shall hire staff but only with presbytery approval.
    e. Membership:
1) The officers elected by the diaconal association shall be the deacon members of the PDC. These officers would normally be a president, secretary, and treasurer. Deacon members shall vote in the committee but not in the presbytery.
2) The elder members are teaching and ruling elders from presbytery.
(Note: BCO 9-5 makes provision for deacons to serve on presbytery committees.)

  2. Form a Presbytery Diaconal Association.
    a. Responsibility for the forming and supervising of the PDA rests with the Presbytery Diaconal Committee.
    b. Membership:
1) All ordained deacons in each member church of the presbytery.
2) Any members of presbytery churches who desire involvement.
    c. Meetings:
1) At first, the association may meet only once or twice a year. The PDC will meet at least quarterly.
2) When the association moves into more advanced stages (see below), an association board should be formed, consisting of a representative from the diaconate of each church, as well as all members of the PDC. At this stage, the board should meet quarterly and the PDC monthly or bi-monthly.

C. Steps of Development.
  1. Fellowship. In its earliest stage, a diaconal association exists to facilitate sharing of hopes, encouragement, burdens, and information. At this stage, an inventory of the gifts and resources of the members of the presbytery's churches should be made.
  2. Education. Deacons meet to receive knowledge and develop skills which will upgrade the performance of their duties.
  3. Need identification. Certain members of the association develop skills in assessing needs and opportunities for mercy ministry in a given area.

4. Consultation. The PDC and certain members of the association develop skills in analyzing and assessing the work of a diaconate and proposing programs and practices to aid them in their work.
5. Funding. The PDC may begin to aid diaconates by offering funds to help meet particular needs or to begin programs beyond the means of that local church.
6. Sponsoring. The PDC and its association may eventually mount its own programs of mercy, in its own name and under its own supervision.

(Note: In the development of the PDC and its association, the above stages should be moved through in order. It is important not to begin taking on difficult cases of need and ambitious projects before there is adequate training and education.)

D. Possible Programs.
1. Develop presbytery-wide service bank (see articles on "service bank"). Keep a file of Christians in the presbytery who have abilities and gifts useful in diaconal work. Doctors, lawyers, judges, may be willing to offer advice or direct assistance to the needy or volunteers. Businessmen, contractors, or industrialists may be able to help with job placement or give advice to sister churches on building programs and equipment purchases. Sociologists, marketing consultants, and urban planners may be able to help churches with church planting or in their evangelistic outreach. City officials, policemen, building inspectors, craftsmen, electricians, carpenters, and plumbers should all be included in such a bank. The bank should receive requests for aid and should then determine if the local church making the request has sufficient resources to meet the need. If the problem is judged to be too great for the congregation, the service bank could act.
2. Establish a presbytery-wide diaconal fund. All churches could make regular contributions to a fund so that no church, especially the smaller ones, would be without help in times of need. The fund should operate similar to a local deacons' fund.
3. Cooperate to fund and staff diaconal programs. A number of churches together could fund a crisis pregnancy center, a housing renovation project, a low cost clothing store, etc. The most important context for such cooperation would be when a denomination has several suburban, middle-class congregations in the same metropolitan area as some inner city churches. The inner city church needs to do diaconal ministry to reach its neighbors.

DISCUSSION QUESTION:

How could your deacons encourage the establishment of a diaconal association in your presbytery? What existing standing committee of presbytery could be approached?

ACTION PLAN

1. What are the most important things which you have learned from this article? List them.

2. Select two or three things which you would like to see put into practice in your church? Name them.

3. In order to implement these, do you need:
   ____ More or better information (about a program, your church, your community, etc.)? What is it?
   ____ More or better skills (abilities, expertise, etc.)? What are they?
   ____ More or better support from key people? Who are they?
   ____ More or better resources (such as money, facilities, personnel, etc.)? What are they?

4. Make a brief plan for securing each of the elements you lack. How could you get information, develop skills, win people's support, raise funds, and so on?

RESOURCES FOR DEACONS

Needs and Programs For Diaconal Ministry

Programs for the Poor

The following are examples of ministries which churches have initiated to care for the needs of the poor.

I. **Emergency Needs**
   A. A Deacons' Fund. This is a substantial sum of money to be used strictly for mercy needs. See separate article on this subject, page 48.
   B. Food "Cupboard" or "Pantry." High protein food is accumulated for free distribution for people in a time of crisis or for people whose income and welfare support are inadequate to feed them properly. Volunteers collect food through periodic "offerings." Families may be challenged to give a can of food a month. Cash donations may be made to an account which supplies perishables (milk, bread). Food may also be obtained by making agreements with local markets or food processing plants to supply food free or at a very low cost. Another source of food is gardening; the church could use part of their property as a garden to produce food for the cupboard.

   Be sure to set up proper "connections." Cooperate with other social relief agencies so they can refer emergency needs to you. Another possibility is to advertise the cupboard in low-rental housing, senior citizen housing, at thrift shops, and wherever people of very limited means will read about it.

   Rather than having "hours," have the cupboard in the church so that a member of the staff can use it to serve people as they come. It is important to ascertain that users are not just middle class "bargain hunters." Also, if a family uses the cupboard several times, be sure to counsel with them to be sure they are making plans or progress to support themselves.

There are many good publications explaining how one church or a number of churches can operate a food cupboard. Read: **Publications List: Community Organizing to End Hunger,** The Children's Foundation, Suite 614, 1028 Connecticutt Ave., N.W., Washington, D.C. 20036.

C. Clothing Closet. Clean and mended clothing is distributed free in much the same way as the food cupboard above is organized. The same principles apply. Volunteers must 1) collect the clothing, 2) sort, repair, and fold/hang clothes in an accessible order.

Before beginning such a project, survey the community to be sure there is a need. Many, many, organizations distribute used clothing. Ordinarily, there is a good supply of clothing in a locality.

D. Housing Assistance. Emergency shelter is often needed for a variety of reasons. A family may be unable to pay rent because of a loss of income or a raise in the rent. In some cases, they may be evicted. Fire or flood can make a house unlivable. So may the negligence of the landlord. People may be in town (for example, to be with a hospitalized family member) and their financial resources have run out. Churches need to heed the biblical call to show hospitality to strangers.

Churches have several options: 1) Have a working relationship with landlords, people who rent rooms, or local motels. When there is a need, deacons go to the landlord, and pay the rent for a needy person or family. 2) Have a network of families within the church who can provide housing for persons in need. 3) Buy a house to be used by the church partially or exclusively for housing needy persons. 4) Have some deacons work as "advocates" to get landlords to maintain the living units more adequately. Advocates could also provide rent subsidies for needy families to avoid their eviction.

For more on diaconal ministry through hospitality, read **Open Heart, Open Home** by Karen Mains (David C. Cook) and **Radical Hospitality** by David Rupprecht.

E. Referral and/or Service Hotline. The church can advertise a phone number offering help for people with physical needs. When someone calls the number, a volunteer refers the caller to an agency in the community which can meet their need. If the church is so equipped, the volunteer connects some group or person in the church who can meet the need. For more information, write: **Referral and Follow-up Program,** National Easter Seal Society, 2023 West Ogden Ave., Chicago, Ill. 60012 and FISH International, 29 Commonwealth Ave., Boston, MA 02116.

F. Transportation Service. Church volunteers may provide their time and vehicles for families who need transportation but who cannot afford any. The elderly are prime examples of people with this need. Deacons will determine what kinds of trips qualify (such as, transportation to the doctor, to a supermarket, etc.). The church then contacts local doctors, pastors, social workers, to tell them of the service and to ask for referrals. Be sure to investigate the implications for insurance coverage!

For more information, ask for the publication, "How to Begin the Senior Adult Transportation Ministry" from

> Mission Support Section
> Baptist General Convention of Texas
> Baptist Building
> Dallas, Texas 75201

II. Developmental Needs

A. Food Store. A church or group of churches may run a store, seasonally or year round, that sells food to the poor at extremely low prices. This is a better ministry than a food closet for a major metropolitan area where there are many more needs. The food store must be located in a poor neighborhood, safe from middle class bargain hunters. The money made through sales can pay rent for the building and utilities.

The Sojourner's Fellowship in Washington, D.C. has operated such a store. For information, write the Fellowship at 1308 L. St. NW, Washington, D.C. 20005.

B. Clothing Store. A church or group of churches may run a store which sells used clothing along the same lines as a food store. Read comments above under I.C. on used clothing programs. Other variations on a clothing ministry are possible. For example, First Baptist Church of Eagle Butte, S.D., provided a complete set of clothing for every newborn baby on the local Indian reservation.

C. Housing. Besides the need for emergency shelter, there is a need for adequate housing at a reasonable price in many poor sections of cities. Some churches have, individually or in groups, bought up, restored, and rented housing to low income families. By offering reasonable rates, and by organizing Bible studies and other ministries within the rental complexes, a Christian witness of word and deed is maintained. In metropolitan New York City, Southern Baptist individuals under the coordination of the Home Missions director, formed a non-profit organization called TONE to do this very thing. Individuals of a PCA church in St. Louis, Missouri, have formed Cornerstone Corporation, which has a similar ministry.

A variation on this ministry is to restore and repair the living quarters of low income persons. The Church of the Savior in Washington, D.C., has had a mission group called "Restoration Corps" which is composed of craftsmen who donate their labor to do this work in the slums of the city. Write these churches for more information on these ministries: The Church of the Savior, 1825 Massachusetts Ave., Washington, D.C., and Grace and Peace Fellowship, 6003 Kingsburg Ave., St. Louis, MO 63112.

D. Job Training and Placement. See page 115.
E. Financial Counseling. See page 117.
F. Medical Clinics. In an emergency, the needy are usually able to get medical care through ordinary channels. However, many of the elderly and poor do not receive adequate check-ups and maintenance health care because the fees of a regular doctor's office visit are too high for their means. Public health departments in a given area may or may not be adequate. With the help of the Red Cross, the local health department, or of sympathetic doctors and medical personnel, many churches have established permanent or periodic free health clinics. Church of the Savior has had such a clinic in a poor neighborhood of Washington, D.C., which has a high rate of health problems.

Clinics may be general or specialized. If there is a particular health need in the area a specialized clinic may be best. "Well Baby" clinics help young unwed or single mothers. Blood pressure and diabetes clinics help the elderly.

G. Community Visitation. Several church workers each adopt a city block in a depressed neighborhood, visiting door-to-door to develop relationships, looking for diaconal needs, and offering help.

For a full description of how to set up such a program, read:

>Block Captain System
>Idea Series No. 1
>Evangelism Dept.,
>Board of Home Ministries
>2850 Kalamazoo Ave., SE
>Grand Rapids, Michigan 49508

H. Economic Cooperatives. A cooperative is an economic structure in which people who need a service own the service organization which they patronize. Cooperatives differ from corporations in a number of key ways: 1) Corporations exist to serve the public for the profit; cooperatives exist to serve its members at cost. 2) Corporations are controlled by money, with each share getting one vote; cooperatives are controlled by people, with each member getting one vote. 3) In corporations, profits are paid to the stockholder in proportion to holdings; in cooperatives, surplus earnings are distributed to members in proportion to patronage.

In poor communities, cooperatives can be enormously helpful for two reasons. 1) The cooperative can provide goods and services to the poor at a reachable price. 2) Usually, the persons who own businesses do not live in poor communities, and thus the profits of a business leave the community. With cooperatives, the money made by the business stays in the community to build personal income, savings, and capital, to create more jobs, and so on. 3) Cooperatives owned by the needy themselves create self-sufficiency. They create the incentive for the poor to develop professional skills. Cooperatives decrease the out-migration from poor communities and can improve overall social and economic conditions.

Anyone in America can form a cooperative. To begin one takes capital and certain types of expertise. Churches sensitive to community needs can provide the start up help to form coops in depressed communities. There may be a need for a housing coop, food coop, farming supplies coop, drug store coop, credit union, and so on.

Such an undertaking is a large and ambitious one. A great deal of study will be necessary. Read: J. H. Cogswell, **The Church and the Rural Poor,** (John Knox Press) and write Voice of Calvary Ministries, 1655 St. Charles St., Jackson, Miss. 39209.

I. Literacy Programs. There is a great need, especially in some communities, for tutoring disadvantaged youth and illiterate or non-English speaking adults.

    Write: Laubach Literacy, Inc.
            Box 131,
            Syracuse, N.Y. 13201

            The Tutor's Handbook
            Voluntary Resources Division
            United Planning Organization
            1021 Fourteenth St., NW
            Washington, D.C. 20005

J. Community Centers. A great variety of educational, recreational and cultural programs can be offered through a community center established in a depressed community. Read: **Community Involvement,** Idea Series No. 16, Christian Reformed Board of Home Missions.

DISCUSSION QUESTIONS:

On the basis of your church's resources and the needs of your community:

1. Which of these ministries would you like to develop soon?
2. Which of these ministries would you like to develop eventually?

APPLICATION:

1. Choose two programs in which you have some interest.

2. Research the programs. Write or visit any church, national or local organizations or other agency which is doing the program or a similar one.
3. Write an initial plan for the program. (See article on "Mercy Ministry Planning Worksheet" page 59.)
4. Draw up an organizational outline, including: a) operating procedure and policies, b) job descriptions, c) standards for evaluating effectiveness, d) pre-service and in-service training.
5. Now do a feasibility study to determine whether your church has the resources for such a program. Estimate: a) skilled and unskilled personnel required, b) man-hours required, c) finances required, d) facilities required, e) attitudes on the part of the congregation required.
6. Have you got what it takes?

    Can you get what it takes? How? By when?

    Could you better do this in cooperation with other churches?

Resettling Refugees

THE URGENT NEED
John H. Skilton, Ph.D.
(May, 1980)

One million people, it is estimated, have fled from communist oppressed Vietnam, Laos, and Cambodia since 1975. Probably from twenty to sixty per cent of those who have escaped from Vietnam by boat have perished in their effort to find refuge. 40,000 of the Hmong people of Laos have escaped to Thailand, and in all likelihood an equal number have died in the attempt. 60,000 Laotians, it would seem, have been sent to government camps, and 200,000 others have escaped to Thailand. The communist regime in Vietnam has apparently followed a program to rid itself of the more than a million ethnic Chinese among its people. Anywhere from one to three million Cambodians have lost their lives under communist savagery, and five million others are now dependent on heroic international efforts to keep them from starving.

Multitudes of refugees in crowded camps in Southeast Asia need to be resettled. If they are not admitted to other countries, many of them may be sent back to face death in the lands from which they have fled.

THE CHRISTIAN MUST ACT

The Christian cannot ignore the despoiled and homeless people of Southeast Asia. He must be like the Samaritan in our Lord's parable (Luke 10:30-37). He has, of course, a special responsibility to Christians among the refugees, for our Saviour identifies himself with them in a special way (Matt. 25:31-46), but he is called upon to do good to all men, including non-Christians (Gal. 6:10), and he finds his neighbor in anyone who is in need (Luke 10:36-37). God's people should have a unique understanding of the plight of the sojourner and the alien (Deut. 10:18-19; I Pet. 1:1; 2:11). The Christian must not let the refugees die. He must show to them the love of the Saviour.

WHAT THE CHRISTIAN CAN DO

Here are some of the things that the Christian can do.
1. PRAY earnestly for the refugees and for wisdom as to how best to help them.
2. SPONSOR refugees. Churches, families, and other groups of Christians can aid in the resettlement of refugees by becoming sponsors. In so doing they assume certain moral, not legal, responsibilities. These responsibilities include welcoming the refugees at a nearby airport, obtaining living quarters for them, providing furniture, bedding, clothing, cutlery, kitchenware, and an initial food supply, arranging for physical and dental examinations and care, introducing them to a culture strange to them, making provision for language instruction, schooling, and em-

ployment, and when feasible arranging for them to receive public assistance, food stamps, and free medical and dental care. Sponsors should in word and deed show the love of Christ to the refugees and should invite them to services of Christian worhsip. Scriptures, tracts, and tapes in the languages of Southeast Asia should be provided.

To sponsor refugees, a first step in the United States is to get in touch with one of the national voluntary agencies working with the U.S. Department of State which are authorized to handle matters connected with the initial resettlement of refugees. Among these agencies are: (1) World Relief Services (a division of the National Association of Evangelicals), P.O. Box WRC, Nyack, NY 10960 (914-353-0640). T. Grady Mangham is in charge of this agency. Services are not restricted to those affiliated with N.A.E. (2) The Lutheran Immigration and Refugee Service, 360 Park Avenue South, New York, NY 10010 (800-223-7656 or 7657). Ask for Mrs. Ingrid Waller. In Philadelphia, call the Lutheran Children and Family Service, 2900 Queen Lane, Philadelphia, PA 19129 (215-951-6850), and ask for Pastor Robert Nelson or Dorrie Sillman. Non-Lutherans are welcome to make use of this service.

The national voluntary agencies provide various types of aid to sponsors. The Lutheran Children and Family Service, for example, affords the assistance of a bilingual staff, translation and language help and guidance, information about housing and employment opportunities, social service aid, special legal assistance, information about the history and customs of countries in Southeast Asia, and a brochure on sponsorship. It can aid the sponsor, when necessary, in obtaining public assistance, food stamps, and medical and dental aid for the refugees. Training programs and manuals are available for those who would teach English as a second language to refugees, and in some places courses in English suited to the needs of refugees are offered. For information about educational and other resources open to sponsors and refugees, consult the Skilton House, 930 W. Oleny Avenue, Philadelphia, PA 19141 (215-924-2426).

Scriptures, tracts, and tapes in the languages of Southeast Asia can be obtained from a number of organizations. For a listing of currently available materials, write American Bible Society, 1865 Broadway, New York, NY 10023; the Gideons International, 2900 Lebanon Road, Nashville, TN 37214; the American Scripture Gift Mission, 1211 Arch Street, Philadelphia, PA 19107; World Relief Refugee Services, P.O. Box WRC, Nyack, NY 10960; and the Far East Broadcasting Company, P.O. Box 1, La Mirada, CA 90637.

3. FOSTER CHILD CARE. For information about this program get in touch with the Lutheran Immigration and Refugee Service, 360 Park Avenue South, New York, NY 10010 (800-223-7656), and ask for Nancy Long.

4. ADOPTION OF CHILDREN. The **Cambodian Action Update** for May 2, 1980 (pp. 7-8) reported that 200 Lao, Khmer, Hmong, and Vietnamese children in refugee camps in Thailand are prospects for adoption. For additional information, call or write the Cambodia Crisis Center, 1523 L Street NW, 6th Floor, Washington, DC 20005 (202-347-4910).
5. HELP PREVENT STARVATION in Cambodia. Contributions can be channeled through churches or diaconal committees such as the Committee on Diaconal Ministries of the Orthodox Presbyterian Church, c/o Rev. Lester R. Bachman, 806 Dorsea Road, Lancaster, PA 17601, or sent directly to Food for the Hungry, Box E, Scottsdale, Arizona 85252; World Vision International, P.O. Box O, Pasadena, CA 91109, or World Relief Refugee Services, P.O. Box WRC, Nyack, NY 10960. To volunteer medical or other services, consult the agencies just mentioned or the Lutheran Immigration and Refugee Service mentioned earlier.
6. ASSISTING REFUGEES ALREADY SETTLED. Many refugees who do not have church sponsorship are in need of assistance of various types, and churches that have sponsored families may welcome additional help. For suggestions call the Skilton House, 930 W. Olney Avenue, Philadelphia, PA 19141 (215-924-2426).
7. Christians can *publicize the need* that exists and recommend appropriate action. Reports, filmstrips, a motion picture, and slides are available, and at times talks and conferences can be arranged. For help in these matters, call the Skilton House (215-942-2426).

On the pedestal of the Statue of Liberty in New York Harbor are inscribed the moving words by Emma Lazarus:

> ... Give me your tired, your poor, your huddled masses yearning to breathe free ... Send these, the homeless, tempest-tost to me ...

We in the United States would like the boat people and the others who have hazarded everything to be free — we would like them all to hear these words. We wish for them the earthly asylum and freedom which the Statue of Liberty symbolizes. But above all we wish for them a more excellent kind of freedom. We wish for them the freedom wherewith Christ has made His people free. We wish that they might all know the truth and that the truth might make them free indeed. We pray that they may hear the Saviour of the world calling: "Come unto me, all ye that labor and are heavy laden, and I will give you rest." We pray that the destitute, hungry, suffering, unwanted, unloved boat people and other refugees may hear the invitation of our loving GOD:

> Ho, every one that thirsteth, come ye to the waters, and he that hath no money, come ye, buy, and eat; yea, come buy wine and milk without money and without price (Isa. 55:1).

Needs of the Elderly

I. **The Growth of the Problems**
   A. The number of the aged is growing steadily. Whereas 4% of the U.S. population was over 65 in 1900, it is well over 10% today, and it will be 20-25% within three decades, as the "baby boom" generation (those born from 1945-1962) move toward old age. Medical advances are also increasing the average life expectancy. Therefore, the number of elderly will grow dramatically.
   B. The problems of the elderly are being aggravated by our modern industrialized society. In more primitive cultures, ownership of farm land was the primary source of power, and the elderly often were those owners. Also, the elderly were respected as having a valuable storehouse of knowledge and expertise concerning farming, crafts, and life in general.

   Our society has reversed this trend. Not land, but a marketable job-skill is a source of wealth. The elderly find themselves untrained and unemployable. The "knowledge explosion" and technological advance make textbooks in most fields dated in five years. The elderly feel useless and ignorant. Lastly, industrialization has made us a mobile society. Many of the elderly find themselves with few or no children and relatives living even in the same state. Neighborhoods experience rapid turnover and so the support system of elderly residents is weakened.
   C. Americans seem to actually fear growing old more than most cultures. We idolize youth, newness, change, personal and sexual attractiveness. Many younger and middle aged Americans simply dislike older persons in general. This distaste cannot only be sensed by the elderly, but, having been infected with it in their own youth, many may now feel it toward themselves.

II. **Specific Needs and Problems**
   A. Adjustment to Physical Limitations.
      1. **Senescense** (not **senility**) is the loss in old age of bodily elasticity. This leads to loss of strength and coordination, decreased circulation, a decrease in mental sharpness, and "chronic" illnesses such as heart disease, high blood pressure, diabetes, and arthritis.
      2. As a result, the elderly need increased health care maintenance. They need to be helped to accept the difficult but major life style changes which are now necessary. Many accustomed activities will have to be eliminated. (One major example is that many elderly cannot or should not drive.) Fear of further disability prompt many of the elderly to psychosomatic illnesses.

B. Adjustment to Economic Limitations.
1. Figures differ due to varying definitions, but 20-30% of the elderly live under the poverty level. The black elderly are even worse off. Some estimate that 90% of all single black females over 65 live in poverty. In 1980, the author knew an aged black woman whose total retirement income was $40.00 a month.
2. Two major influences which crush the elderly economically are inflation and health care costs. To older persons having two or more chronic health conditions, medical costs are staggering. Just when the elderly need more money than ever to meet such expenses, there is a drastic reduction of income.
3. The elderly are in need of financial and business advice to handle matters such as income tax, will, insurance and government aid programs. These matters are complex and new to the older persons who deal with them.

C. Adjustment to Social Changes.
1. The elderly in today's industrialized society have no clearly defined place or usefulness. The retired male, in particular, must grapple with a feeling of uselessness. For years, long hours of work have consumed all his attention. He may have developed few outside interests. Those who have done primarily manual work may now be unable to perform the tasks which make him feel useful. Boredom and depression set in.
2. The retired person must face the loss of many friends and relatives by death. Most difficult of all is the loss of a spouse. A newly single woman must face responsibilities she has never had in 50 years of marriage; the newly single man must do the same. Long-time friends and spouses are socially irreplaceable. Many surviving elderly respond by becoming lonely and isolated.
3. Old age complicates one's relationship to one's children. Because of our mobile society and the breakdown of the extended family, many of the aged live alone and are distant from their children. Also, the increased emphasis on affluence and comfort has weakened younger Americans' toleration for personal and economic sacrifice. A conservative estimate is that one-third of all nursing home residents could be living at home with support from the family. On the other hand, children concerned to help may be opposed by parents who cannot live alone but who insist on doing so. Such conflicts strain relationships and further isolate the elderly person.

D. Adjustment to Spiritual Problems.
1. Fear of death casts its shadow over the thinking of many of the elderly. Grief over the death of loved ones mixes with fear of one's own death to make a powerful depressant. Consider how many elderly people must go to a funeral of a friend, neighbor, relative or associate, nearly every month.
2. Closely related to this can be a sense of guilt or regret over past mistakes or wasted opportunities which may burden them. In busier years, such matters could be repressed, but now they are "ever before them."
3. Worry about family members and about their own health and condition plague those whose minds are not regularly occupied. Psychosomatic illnesses are the result.
4. Self-pity and introspection come from the loneliness and sense of uselessness that comes with age. Many of the aged who seem pre-occupied may lose hearing and memory of the immediate past and even the present, not because of physical deterioration, but as a way of escape from unpleasant reality.

III. **Meeting Needs of Older Persons.** (See also next article.)
A. Physical — Provide the support necessary to help with physical adjustments.
1. Provide financial help for medical bills. This will ease anxieties. Free, basic health care could be provided. For example, a nurse from the church could take blood pressure periodically.
2. Provide new programs which teach hobbies or offer activities more in accord with a lifestyle tailored to physical limitations.
3. Give diaconal support to enable the elderly to stay in their homes. For example, provide transportation for those who cannot drive. Provide yardwork or home maintenance for those who cannot do certain chores, etc.
4. Show consideration for the physical limitations of the elderly by reserving seating spaces and parking spaces for them, by offering communion in the homes of shut-ins and taking them sermon cassettes, by putting large-print books for the church library, etc.
B. Economic.
1. Provide financial subsidies for the elderly. Keep in mind their need for self-respect. Be creative in ways to help them "make ends meet."
2. Offer free or low cost hot meals at the church regularly.

Have families of the church bring the elderly into their homes for meals regularly. Provide financial counseling by finance professionals in the church. Provide church owned and operated apartments at a lower cost.

C. Social.
1. Help the elderly to cope with loneliness, by having families "adopt a grandparent," by creating social groups within the church for them, by providing a "drop in center" at the church for them, by having church youth and others involved regular visitation of the elderly, by telephoning regularly, etc.
2. Help the elderly to retire to new work, not to total recreation. The Bible does not say "work six days until you retire!" Older persons need to be given part-time jobs and volunteer opportunities. (See following article for examples.)
3. Be sure to minimize the feeling of neglect by giving the elderly a voice in church government and in worship.
4. Provide seminars on retirement, dealing with government agencies, budgeting, and other issues of interest to the aged.
5. Provide counseling to help the elderly cope with grief.

D. Spiritual — All the elderly's problems are in the final sense spiritual. The aged person must come to grips with the sovereignty of God, who has said that he leads us into old age, but will sustain us there, in the midst of the limitations and grief (Isa. 46:4).

Note: Following is an outline of Scripture and methods of spiritual care to be used for elderly persons with different needs. Only the first heading, anxiety, is presented in full. The minister of mercy who would meet needs should fill out his own notebook under each heading.

1. For anxiety:
   a. Understand worry. Worry is excessive concern which needs to be channeled into two activities. 1) Planning and work. Often, there is so much to be done that the matter is worried about (Matt. 6:34). 2) Prayer with thanksgiving. Often worry is over a matter about which the person can do nothing. In such a case, worry is a lack of submission to God's will (Phil. 4:6ff.).
   b. Make a plan.
      (1). If your problem is a lack of planning and work, sit down and plan what you will do about it. Schedule it. Then don't think about it until it is time to act.

(2). If your problem is mainly a lack of faith in God, confess to God that you are insulting his wisdom and power. Pray about the matter briefly and thank God ahead of time for what he is going to do. Then turn to other jobs and duties. Get busy.
    c. Other Scripture passages: Proverbs 12:25; 14:30; 17:22; 28:1; Matthew 6:24-34; Luke 8:14; 10:38-42; James 4:13ff.; I Peter 5:6-7.

2. For grief:
   a. Help the person through the initial stage of disruption. During the time of shock, simply provide a listening ear and your presence.
   b. Help the person through the longer period of regrouping. Using I Thessalonians 4:13 show that grief is right, but it can become sinful despair if Christian hope is not focused on.
   c. Scriptures: Psalm 23, 42, 31: 9 ff., 77; Proverbs 14:13; 15:13; 16:1, 3; 17:22; John 11; II Corinthians 1; 4; Philippians 4:13.

3. For loneliness:
   a. There is no need to be ashamed of loneliness. Adam was lonely even when he was without sin. See Genesis 2:18-25.
   b. Therefore, although you may have lost many old friends, you need to make new ones. You must remember how that is done. Listen. Be kind. Be open about your thoughts and feelings. Invite others to do things with you. Don't be possessive. On the qualities of a friend: Proverbs 14:20; 19:4, 6, 7; 17:17; 18:24; 27:10 (constancy), 27:6; 29:5; 28:23 (candor), 27:9, 17 (counsel), 25:17; 27:14; 25:20; 26:18, 19 (tact).
   c. Clear out other problems which may be causing isolation. Guilt, bitterness against others, bitterness against God, self-pity all aggravate loneliness. Scriptures: Romans 8:28; 5:3-5; Hebrews 12:1-15; James 1:1-2; Proverbs 12:18; 16:18, 28; 17:9, 13-14, 18-20; Psalm 51; Matthew 5:21, 22.
   d. Strengthen your friendship with God. Scriptures: John 14:23; 15:14-15.
   e. Do not simply attend church. Become involved in a class or group (Heb. 10:24-25).

4. For guilt:
   a. Confess the sin to God without blameshifting. (1) Think first of the danger of your sin, what troubles it has and can bring you. (2) Think next of the guilt of your sin, what ingratitude it is to God (Ps. 51).
   b. Confess your sin to anyone you have wronged (Matt. 5:21, 22).
   c. Make a plan to change so that the sin will not as likely occur again (Luke 3:10:14).
   d. Thank God for his provision for your sin. Do not continue in self-criticism. You are forgiven for Jesus' sake (I John 1:8-10; 2:1).
   e. Other Scriptures: Isaiah 1:18; 53:5-6; Hebrews 4:14-16.
5. For self-pity:
   a. Remember that no one has ever gotten what he or she deserves. We deserve nothing! Everything we have is a free gift (I Cor. 4:7).
   b. Consider the things we have permanently that are more valuable than anything we can lose. Salvation (Heb. 10:22, 35-36; I John 3:18-22), Heaven (Ps. 16; Rev. 21; I Peter 1), God's presence, guidance, love, care (Matt. 5:5, 6; 6:24-34; Phil. 4:6-12; John 15:12-17).
   c. See how the psalmist handled self-pity in Psalm 73. See how Paul could always stay content in Philippians 3:7-11 and 4:10-13.
   d. THE MOST IMPORTANT ANTIDOTE TO SELF-PITY, AND TO DEPRESSION IN GENERAL, IS TO SERVE SOMEONE ELSE (Isa. 58:10).
6. For fear of death:
   a. If the person is a Christian, simply share the promises of eternal life with him. Encourage him to meditate on heaven and these promises: Philippians 1:19-26; II Corinthians 4:16-5:9; John 14; Romans 8:18-39; I Corinthians 15:54-58.
   b. If the person is not a Christian, share the gospel. See especially C. John Miller, "Witnessing to the Dying."
   c. If the person is a Christian, he may lack assurance of salvation because of a guilty conscience. Encourage him to clear his conscience with Psalm 51; Luke 15; I John 1:8-10 and 2:1.

7. For general discouragement in the face of suffering see full article below on "How to Handle Suffering."

FOR FURTHER STUDY:

Tom and Penny McCormick, **Nursing Home Ministry: A Manual** (Great Commission Publications).

Robert Gray and David Moberg, **The Church and the Older Person** (Eerdmans).

Report of the Committee on Senior Ministry, Christian Reformed Board of Home Missions (1985) an excellent resource.

DISCUSSION:

Consider some people you know who are elderly. What physical, economic, social, and spiritual needs do they have? What sorts of ministries could the church provide to meet them?

PROJECTS:

1. Ask a pastor or an officer of another church with a solid program for senior adults to speak to your board, describing the program and its benefits.
2. Interview several elderly church members. Ask at least the following questions: What are the worst problems senior adults face? In what ways is the church serving you now? In what way is it failing to serve you? What suggestions do you have for the church so that it could serve you better?

Programs for the Elderly

I. **Varieties of Ways to Help the Elderly**
   A. Hot Lunches. Meals are provided at the church or taken to homes ("Meals on Wheels").
   B. Friendly Visitor Program. Trained volunteers regularly visit the elderly in their homes or in the nursing home. The purpose is to supply the social, emotional, and spiritual support and care which the elderly need. Often, social workers can provide the church with numbers of lonely elderly people in your locale. Also contact the directors of senior housing units or senior citizen organizations. You will get many names and addresses.

   > Note: Accompanying or growing out of the friendly visitor program will be other helping ministries. Some of these are listed below.

   C. Housekeeper-helper Program. Volunteers in this program must be willing to give an amount of time each week to provide domestic services to those elderly who have physical limitations. This is not meant to provide professional nursing care to senior adults who need that kind of help.
   D. Transportation Ministry. See a description above under "Programs for the Poor". Weekly, elderly people can be provided free transportation to the market, bank, and any other important appointment (such as a doctor's visit).
   E. Telephone Reassurance Program. This program provides a call every day or periodically to an elderly person living alone.
   F. Retired Persons Employment Registry. Several national organizations utilize the volunteer help of senior adults to perform community services. Foster Grandparents, Service Corps of Retired Executives, and the Retired Senior Volunteer Program (RSVP) all offer excellent service opportunities for older persons. (Note: Single federal agency coordinates these efforts.) A church may set up such programs. It may help retired persons get part time jobs. It may connect the retired person's skills with needs in the church.
   G. Health Care Services. Provide a free medical clinic which focuses on the health needs of the elderly. Provide home health care with some volunteer health professionals.
   H. Housing Help. Provide volunteers who can do repair and maintenance to the homes of the elderly. Buy and rent low-cost housing to the elderly.
   I. Educational Services. The elderly need guidance on many issues, including retirement planning, estate planning, legal services for the elderly, filling out Medicare forms, health care and fitness, learning new hobbies and interests, facing grief, safety, etc.

J. Day Care Center for the Elderly. Many older persons living with their families can avoid nursing homes by spending eight hours a day at a day care center. Staff can help them learn developmental skills and give attention to physical and emotional needs. This service is a special ministry to those families who care for aging relatives.

K. Recreation/"Drop In Center". People come to play cards, read newspapers and periodicals, learn a variety of crafts and skills, register for outings and various bus trips, and discuss problems with a counselor.

II. **A Variety of Jobs for the Elderly in the Church**

A. Telephone Ministry. Let the elderly visit the sick by phone, or help the church staff with administrative tasks.

B. Child Care Ministry. By helping in nurseries, with other church child care ministries, by babysitting for young couples, or by serving as substitute grandparents (especially for children living with only one parent), senior adults can minister, using skills of child care they learned as parents.

C. Prayer Ministry. Challenge the senior adults to serious, prevailing prayer. Set up prayer chains. Get commitments to set times and hours of prayer for specific needs. Have retired persons active in prayer share answered prayers in the congregation. Schedule regular prayer groups.

D. Other Ministries: Secretarial, janitorial, educational.

FOR FURTHER READING:

"How to Begin the Church Senior Adult Club Program",
"How to Begin the Senior Adult Transportation Ministry",
and "How to Begin the Telephone Reassurance Ministry."
Obtain from:
    Missions Support Section
    Baptist General Convention of Texas
    Baptist Building,
    Dallas, Texas 75201

Report of The Committee on Senior Ministry
Christian Reformed Board of Home Missions
2850 Kalamazoo Ave.
Grand Rapids, Michigan 49560

Robert J. Burns, **A Program for Older Adults in the Church,** (Baker)

Horace Kerr, **How to Minister to the Senior Adults in Your Church,** (Broadman)

Gray and Moberg, **The Church and The Older Person,**
    (see especially chapters 6-9)

PROJECTS:
1. Fill out the "Checklist for a Congregation's Ministries with and for the Aging" on page 22 of the CRC's Report of the Committee on Senior Ministry.
2. On the basis of what you know about your community's needs and your church's resources, decide which of the programs you would like to see begin.
3. Appoint a task force on senior adult ministry to study the needs of the elderly and return with recommendations.

Nursing Home Ministry

For a church to make a lasting impact on the lives of nursing home residents, there is a need for the church to develop a carefully planned, comprehensive program. Sporadic, thinly-manned efforts will reap little fruit.

I. **Initiation**
   A. Be sure to discover all the nursing homes in your area. Remember, they may not all be called "nursing homes", but rather "convalescent centers" and so on.
   B. Before contacting any institutions, read and study all of the materials on ministry to the elderly. Assess the gifts and resources of your church. Have an inventory of programs which you believe you could perform.
   C. Contact the director and the activities director if there is one. Explain your goals. Present what you are capable of doing. Ask about the specific needs of the institution and seek to agree on a program that matches your resources to their needs.
   D. If permission is granted to begin, be sure to meet all the responsible people in the administration of the institution.

II. **Visitation**
   The "backbone" of any nursing home ministry, regardless of the various kinds of programs possible, is visitation. Volunteers must be able to relate personally to nursing home residents.
   A. Visitors must be trained in such subjects as:
      1. The process of aging (perhaps taught by a nursing home staff member).
      2. The problems of the handicapped and chronically ill elderly; how to deal with the hearing impaired, the visually impaired, senile, etc. (perhaps taught by a nurse).
      3. Community resources for the elderly (perhaps taught by a social worker or someone from a retired persons' association).
      4. The use of the Scripture and prayer to meet spiritual needs (taught by a pastor).
      5. The art of listening and conversing; details of what to do on the first and on subsequent visits (perhaps taught by an experienced layperson).
   B. Visitors should be volunteers who are willing to devote one morning, afternoon, or evening a week.

III. **Worship**
   A. One of the most important things your church can do is sponsor a

regular worship service. If the home already has one manned by a local council or churches, you may be allowed to sponsor another one weekly on some other day.

B. Assign this duty to an interested group within the church (a committee of deacons, a women's association, etc.). A committee of four people could serve as coordinators, with each person coordinating one service a month. The coordinator's job would include:
1. Setting up the room.
2. Recruiting some church members to come and worship with the other church members.
3. Going out with other volunteers to invite members to the service.
4. Arranging for music and a speaker/worship leader.

C. The speaker should plan the service and be sure to adapt to the audience. Sermons should be 10 minutes long and filled with illustrations. The delivery should be very animated with lots of variation in tone of voice. He must speak loudly, slowly, clearly. If possible, the illustrations should be acted out by church members. Hymns should be old favorites. Preaching themes should be on gratitude, praise, hope, and submission to God's will. The aged need to be fortified against self-pity and self-centeredness.

IV. **Activities**

A. It may be useful to approach the activities director of the nursing home and ask what needed activities there are that the church could help with. There is an infinite variety of social, cultural, educational, and recreational programs that could be provided.

B. The coordinator of the church program could set up a schedule for the year and recruit various groups and classes of the church to each assume the responsibility for one or two programs a year.

FOR FURTHER STUDY:

Nursing Home Ministry: A Manual by the McCormicks is the most useful tool available. It lists many other resources.

American Red Cross Friendly Visiting Manual
American Red Cross Volunteer Services
23rd and Chestnut Streets
Philadelphia, PA 19103

Institutional Evangelism (Idea Series No. 18)
Christian Reformed Board of Home Missions

Programs for Disadvantaged Children

Introduction

If conditions were ideal, the church's ministry to children would be through the family. The parents would be equipped to love, teach, and nurture their children in the Lord. But many children have no parents, have one parent, or have parents who are failing in their duties. These are the "helpless" and the "fatherless" that the church is to protect (Jas. 1:27; Ps. 68:5; I Tim. 5:4).

I. **Needs**

   A. Child Abuse and Neglect. Overly harsh physical discipline, failing to provide proper diet, clothing, shelter, or supervision, denial of medical care, or overworking a child are all considered abuse or neglect. Parents who expose children to continued crime, drug use, or prostitution are considered guilty of abuse/neglect as well.

   B. Delinquency. A juvenile delinquent can be defined as a child or youth who is habitually truant from school, who is breaking public laws or ordinances, who associates with criminals, or who is considered out of control of his parents or guardian.

   C. "Culturally Deprivation." Many children are raised in an environment in which they learn few language skills and reading skills. The result is poor school performance. All of these conditions are the result of a lack of parental nurture, due either to the absence, the unwillingness, or the inability of the parents.

II. **Programs and Ministries**

   A. Foster Care. When parents are unwilling or unable to meet the needs of a child at home, the local government determines to place the child in a foster home. Churches can motivate a number of families in the church to commit themselves to foster care. In preparation these couples can meet for study and training; books, films, and speakers should be utilized. After the families take in the children and youths, they would continue to meet together for problem-solving and support, and to plan family social activities.

   A variation on this theme is provided by FLOC (For the Love of Children). This is a mission group of the Church of the Savior in Washington, D.C. It is a placement service which puts foster children in decent homes. It even has worked to purchase and rent homes for some families to reunite them with their children.

   It is clear that in all cases, the church must work closely with the civil authorities.

B. Schools and Day Care Centers. Churches sensitive to mercy needs will realize that many low income parents who lack nurturing skills need to be working but cannot afford day care. Special subsidies for needy families and a high-quality day care program would be a ministry both to the parents and the children.

C. Adopt a Family. In this ministry, trained members of the church work with troubled families. These families may be in the church or referred to the church through social service departments, child welfare office, or some other government agency. Some variations:

   1. Parent aides. The volunteer helps the parent(s) identify problems, solutions and then to set goals for improvement.
   2. Big brother/sister. The church can work through an existing program or set up their own. The volunteers commit time to build a relationship with a needy youngster.

D. Tutoring. Tutors seek to help children and youth improve their school work. Tutoring programs can be more or less ambitious, depending on the church's resources. College students could be used to help high school dropouts pass the high school equivalency test. Youth and retired persons could be used to help slow students in elementary school. All should be done in association with school authorities.

E. Family Education. Parents can benefit from classes on discipline, nutrition, planning recreation, etc. Deacons can find parents who would benefit from the classes by getting names from local child welfare agencies.

F. Sponsors for Juvenile Offenders. Church volunteers may be able to minister to juvenile offenders at several points in the juvenile court system.

Although local systems may vary, juvenile courts have three main courses of action to take with an offender: 1) unconditionally release him/her, 2) release him/her into a diversionary program run by some social agency, or 3) place him into a detention center to await a hearing. Hearings generally result in: 1) probation under a probation officer, 2) placement in a juvenile rehabilitative institution, 3) placement into the custody of social services and usually a foster home, 4) placement in some other home or institution that works with delinquents.

It is evident that churches can become involved at a number of places in this system. They may offer trained volunteer individuals or families to provide companionship and support to an offender during probation or after release. Churches may establish diversionary programs or temporary shelters for juvenile offenders.

FOR FURTHER STUDY:
> Write: National Program for Voluntary Action
> Paramount Building,
> 1735 "I" St., NW
> Washington, D.C. 20006
> Ask for portfolios on work with juvenile delinquents, tutoring programs, and other work with disadvantaged children.
>
> FLOC
> Church of the Savior, Washington, D.C.

PROJECTS:
1. Interview a child welfare social worker, a school guidance counselor, a juvenile parole officer. Ask them what the greatest problems are of children and youth in your area. Ask what is being done now to help and what your church could do.
2. Choose a program listed in this article. Assign it to a task force which will research it and bring a report on its feasibility back to the deacons soon.

Helping Parents with their Parenting

One of the jobs of those ministering to troubled families will be to help them develop nurturing skills. Here is a basic outline of the skills.

I. **Structure of the Theory**

There are three main components to raising a child. Eph. 6:4 — "Bring them up in the nurture and admonition of the Lord."

A. Relationship ("Admonition").

This is primary. First, parents must develop a strong relationship of communication and love with their child. Without this, you cannot administer discipline or teach values. The elements of building a good relationship are:

1. Affirmation (showing love and affection),
2. Accessibility (spending time; being approachable),
3. Communication.

B. Discipline ("Nurture").

Once a child feels loved and understood, parents must discipline their children toward the goal of wisdom. In Proverbs, a wise man has self-control, knows his own weaknesses and limits, makes decisions based on a long range perspective, and knows how to serve others. Discipline is not simply punishing, it is training for wisdom. The elements of discipline are:

1. Knowing your child,
2. Setting up rules in accordance with the child's nature and needs,
3. Choosing and administering rewards and punishments.

C. Spiritual Formation ("bring them up").

The ultimate goal of child rearing is not merely keeping one's children "in line" (discipline) nor even making them your friends (relationship), but rather bringing them up to maturity of character and the fullness of the stature of Christ. Discipline and love makes discipling possible. Parents aim to produce a person reflecting the character of God. The elements of spiritual formation are:

1. Managing (monitoring a child's experiences and the input into his/her mind),
2. Modeling (by your example),
3. Teaching.

II. **Teaching Ideas**

The following outline is not theory. Instead, it consists of very practical units of thought to be communicated by deacons when discussing child nurture with parents. A deacon should begin by reviewing each principle with the parent, especially the ones that the parent is most evidently lacking in. The second step of aid will be to help the parent make detailed application of the principles that need to be worked on. If there is not progress, then the third step would be to get the family to a Christian counselor.

Step 1 — General teaching principles

1. Watch carefully to catch your children being "good." Don't ignore them when they are behaving well. Fuss over good behavior more than over bad behavior. Try to do so every hour at least.
2. Offer children a routine. Stick to a schedule for bed times, naps, and meals. Don't let a child decide his/her own schedule. Children need the security of structure.
3. Discipline must be absolutely consistent. The same punishment must always follow the same crime. It should be matter of fact. Your attitude should be solemn but not cold and hostile. Be sympathetic but firm. Make discipline quick. A swat or confinement to a chair for three or four minutes is sufficient for preschoolers.
4. Your tongue matters. Do not lecture or nag and threaten. Punish after one warning and them drop the subject.
5. Let your children help you. Many chores too difficult for them to do alone can be occasions for learning and relating if you let them work with you. Make cookies, take out the garbage with them. It will usually make more work for you, of course!
6. Take time off from your children. Don't be too guilt-ridden and/or possessive to get away regularly.
7. Show love to your children in three ways: 1) eye contact, a) physical contact, c) and focused attention. Do not let yourself get into the trap of only talking to your child when you are doing something else. Have at least one-half to one hour of time each day to concentrate just on your children and nothing else. Be sure each child gets some time alone with you each week. Don't just tell them you love them; show them.

Step 2 — Application of principles

At this level, have parents read a book or two from the following list. Choose some appropriate exercises in the book for the parent(s) to do to apply principles and learn nurturing skills.

1. On relationship problems:
   Ross Campbell, **How to Really Love Your Child** (Victor)
   H. N. Wright, **Communication: Key to Your Teens** (Harvest)
2. On discipline problems:
   J. Dobson, **Dare to Discipline** (Tyndale)
   J. Dobson, **The Strong-Willed Child** (Tyndale)

3. On teaching and modeling:
   G. MacDonald, **The Effective Father** (Tyndale)

A Flow Chart for Helping Unwed Mothers

One class of persons with economic needs is the (often young) single pregnant woman. When faced with such a case, ministers of mercy should proceed to give aid along the following lines.

I. Be sure the woman is really pregnant, do not rely on her own "do-it-yourself" tests.

II. Help her choose a course of action. Her alternatives are:

   A. **To have an abortion.** Seek to convince her not to have an abortion. Counsel her that this is not an issue of practicality but of morality. Show her that fetuses in the womb are considered **persons** by God (Gen. 26:22; Job 3:3, Isa. 44:2; 49:5; Hos. 12:3; Ps. 139:13-16) and are capable of being called and filled by the Holy Spirit (Jer. 1:5; Luke 1:34-45). If the pregnant woman's parents counsel abortion, say to them, "Your daughter brought you economic difficulty and embarrassment, but you never killed her to solve it! Neither should this child be killed."

   B. **To give the child up for adoption.**
      1. This decision hinges on: 1) The mother's age and maturity. (Is she able to care for the child?) 2) The grandparent's attitude. (Will their commitment to help their daughter raise the child be necessary? Is that commitment present? 3) The alleged father. (Is he known? Will he press for parental rights? Will he pay to support the child?)
      2. Prepare for adoption: 1) By having the mother remain in her present living situation until the child is born. Then the child can be given to a licensed adoption agency through a juvenile court. Or, 2) By placing the mother with a family or organization which can give her financial and emotional support until the baby is born. One example of such a residential institution is the **Children's Home of Florida** (201 Osceola Ave. at South Palmetto, Daytona Beach, FL 32014, phone 904-255-7407). A different example is **Choose Life, Inc.** of Chattanooga, TN. The mother is placed in the home of a trained Christian family. A local church could train some of its own families for such a ministry.
      3. A Christian adoption agency which will place children in Christian homes is Bethany Christian Services, which has offices across the country. Its headquarters is at 901 Eastern Ave., NE, Grand Rapids, MI 49503 (610-459-6273).

    C. **To raise the child herself.**
        1. This decision hinges on the same questions as the question to adopt.
        2. These are four avenues to take if this option is chosen.
            a) Temporary foster care may be provided for the child, if the mother needs to finish her education and find a job.
            b) Temporary foster care may be provided for the mother and the child together. (If the mother is 18 or older no legal action would be necessary.)
            c) She could raise the child alone with extensive counseling, economic aid and companionship provided by the church.
            d) She could stay with her parents and raise the child there.
    D. **To get married.**
        1. If marriage was not seriously considered before the pregnancy, this is a bad option.
        2. Even if marriage was considered before the pregnancy was discovered: 1) Is there personal maturity sufficient for building a home? 2) Is there an adequate financial base? 3) Is there a loving commitment of both parties to each other? If these factors are lacking, marriage should at least be postponed.
        3. The rights and responsibilities of the unwed father are being shaped and reshaped by courts and legislatures. Be sure to find out the laws of the state.
III. If she has not told her parents, advise her to do so. If she is a minor it is required. If she is not legally dependent on her parents, it is still advisable.
IV. Help her make plans to get good prenatal care. Women under 18 have "high risk" pregnancies.
V. Help her to continue her education through public school classes for pregnant girls, special tutors, or other means available in your community.
VI. Help her plan her next three-five years financially.
    A. Will parents pay all costs? If not:
    B. Find out what government welfare funds are available for prenatal care, delivery and support of the child.
    C. Meet the immediate economic needs through the church. The congregation can provide funds, hospitality, maternity and baby clothes, free day care, while the mother works or finishes school and so on.

	D. Get vocational counseling for her.
VII.	Give her or arrange for her to get counseling on: 1) child-rearing, 2) single living, 3) handling her emotions, 4) evangelism (if necessary).

Read: G. Berghoef and L. DeKoster, **The Elder's Handbook** (Grand Rapids: Christian's Library Press, 1979, chapter 8).

Rose Bernstein, **Helping Unmarried Mothers** (New York: Association Press, 1971).

DISCUSSION QUESTION:

Recall some cases of premarital pregnancy with which you have been familiar. How was the case handled? What was done properly? Improperly? (If you discuss this with a group, be sure to leave the parties nameless.)

Prisoners: Their Problems and the Biblical Solution

I. **The Problems of Prisoners**

In the crowded, brutal, lonely and impersonal setting of a prison, where murders and suicides are routine, inmates experience a number of crying needs:

A. The need for **friendship.** Though the prison destroys privacy, it at the same time creates great loneliness. An inmate experiences harsh treatment both from prison officers and fellow inmates who are trying to survive. Prisoners need someone to "hear them out" and to listen to their frustration.

B. The need for **family bridge-building.** Most prisoners' marital relationships are severely strained and usually broken by incarceration. Inmates can often see but cannot meet the severe economic and emotional needs his imprisonment inflicts on his family.

C. The need for **dignity.** Prison life is dehumanizing. Inmates are stripped of personal items and clothing. The regimentation and boring routine contribute to a sense of overwhelming helplessness. Many escape by sleeping 18-20 hours a day. Others will fantasize. A high percentage of inmates experience mental disturbance, because they are not treated with the dignity which human beings deserve and need.

D. The need for **preparation for re-entry into society.** Besides needing education and job training inside the institution, they require assistance in finding a job and a place to live outside the prison. Re-entry is extremely difficult after the experience of prison life, where all initiative is taken away from the inmate.

E. The need for **advocates.** A prisoner needs help with his legal problems. "Advocates" can give positive references to parole boards, courts, and potential employers.

F. The need for **reconciliation with God.** Fundamentally, all men are under the sentence of God's judgment, regardless of their standing with the civil law.

II. **The Biblical Mandate for Prison Ministry**

A. **Visit Prisoners.**

In Matthew 25:36c, Jesus says, "I was in prison and you visited me." This Greek word *elthate,* differs from another word for "visit" used in verse 36b, *episkepto,* which means "to supervise, to look after." *Elthate* means simply to be present. Christians are to be with prisoners. Consistent effort at befriending prisoners is crucial. Many inmates scorn the "hit and run" prison ministries in which Christians come in for a worship service and the distribution of cookies and then go home until next Christmas! Christians must be present, over the long term, to listen and befriend inmates.

B. **Love Prisoners.**

In Hebrews 13:3, we are told "Remember them in prison as if in prison yourselves." This is a challenge to the deepest kind of understanding toward prisoners. We are to bind our hearts to them so that the joys and hurts of the prisoner become our own. We must treat them with the dignity they deserve as creatures in the image of God. This verse forbids a merely dutiful program of visitation, services, and meetings.

C. **Release Prisoners.**

Luke 4:18 tells us Jesus saw that his ministry included "preaching release to the prisoner." What can this mean? The implication of this text works out on three levels.

1. It means to work for the release of those unjustly imprisoned and/or unfairly kept in prison.
2. It means to release prisoners from the cycle of crime by helping them socially, educationally, vocationally until they never need to return to correctional institutions.
3. It means to preach the gospel to prisoners so that their truest guilt is covered and they are reconciled to the Righteous Judge. When they are righteous in his sight, their spiritual bonds are broken (John 8:36).

These three verses — Matthew 25:36, Hebrews 13:3 and Luke 4:18 — outline an extensive ministry Christians are to have to prisoners. We may not confine our ministry to only mercy needs or only "spiritual needs." We must visit, help, love, rehabilitate, and redeem them, even as God visited us in our bondage and redeemed us.

For further reading: **Prison People: A Guide for Prison Fellowship Volunteers** (copyright Prison Fellowship, P.O. Box 40562, Washington, DC 20016).

DISCUSSION QUESTION:

What would be the problem your church would face if it began a ministry to prisoners?

Guide for Visiting the Sick

I. **Goals for Visitation of the Sick**
   A. To meet spiritual needs which sickness may create or which may actually create sickness.
      1. Sickness may cause or be caused by guilt. A sick person may be sick because of sin.
         a. Sickness may cause guilt. Bitterness, excessive worry (what is often called "nerves"), overwork or other sinful behavior can all cause major physical problems. It is also possible that, though the sickness is not directly caused by a particular sin, the patient is nonetheless made by his helplessness to see his errors. In either case, the sickness helps to convict the patient of his sin. He then needs to resolve to change and be rightly related to God.
         b. On the other hand, sickness may directly be caused by guilt. A person's conscience can make him sick. He needs to clear his conscience and rest in the forgiveness of God.
      2. Sickness may cause anxiety or anger. Frequently sick persons need to be reminded of God's wisdom and of his loving care in all circumstances.
      3. Sickness may cause loneliness. The patient may be cut off from friends and loved ones. He/she may simply need a friendly listener to overcome the loneliness.
      4. Sickness may cause a feeling of meaninglessness. Serious illness may hamper work or other important life goals. Boredom and a sense of uselessness prevail. Sick persons must be shown the opportunities of growth that sickness affords.
   B. To discover physical needs which sickness may create and which the church can meet.
      1. Housekeeping and domestic needs during sickness.
      2. Financial problems due to medical and related costs.
      3. Child care needs.
      4. Sitting with the sick.

II. **Meeting the Needs of the Sick**
   A. Guilt.
      1. Take the person seriously when he makes negative statements about himself. Don't minimize.
      2. Be warm and sympathetic especially when you are calling a sin a sin.

3. Share the gospel with the person if you do not think he or she is a Christian. Do not do so if the person is physically incapable of strong emotions or if the person is under heavy medication.
4. Help him to reconcile with God:
    a. Direct him to stop blaming anyone or anything else for the behavior and to take full responsibility.
    b. Confess the sin to God, not so much for the pain it has caused you, but for the grief and dishonor it has caused him.
    c. If necessary, have him determine to ask forgiveness of any person he has wronged.
    d. Have him thank God for a full payment for sin in Jesus Christ.
    e. Have him make any plans necessary so that the sin is unlikely to occur again.

B. Anxiety and Anger.
(See the full article on "How to Handle Suffering" page 119.)

C. Loneliness.
Be a listener. See below for details.

D. Meaninglessness.
1. Treat the person with respect and dignity, not as a child. Be careful not to treat him as more helpless than he really is.
2. Help him or her to think through alternatives for work and activity if his physical condition makes such changes necessary.
3. Show him the opportunities for Bible study and spiritual growth. (See "How to Handle Suffering" page 119.)

III. Tools for Visitation of the Sick
A. The Bible
1. Principles.
    a. Read the Scripture near the end of the visit. Choose a passage suited to the person's needs. Normally, choose a passage before a visit, but be ready to change.
    b. Choose a passage that expresses the feelings and needs of the patient and which answers the need.
    c. If the person is very sick, or tired, simply read the passage. Otherwise, make also an explanatory remark or two. For example, after reading Matthew 6:25-34 say: "We worry, but this helps, doesn't it? If he takes

care of the birds and grass, doesn't it make sense that he'll take care of you?" Pause to give the person a chance to respond. If he doesn't, open the door again by saying: "That is really great, isn't it?" Seek a discussion on the implications of the verses. If there is no time, apply the verse when you pray: "Lord, we need not worry about our bodies when we remember your powerful loving care. Help Tom to remember and so give him your peace."

2. Practice.
   a. For thanksgiving after illness:
      Ps. 40:1-3; 103; 92:1-4.
   b. On suffering and God's purposes:
      (1) For those in pain: Heb. 4:14-16; 12:1-13; Isa. 40:30-31; 43:1-3; Rom. 8:18; II Cor. 1:3-11; 4; James 1:2-4.

      (2) Benefits of affliction: (Strengthens faith and character) Deut. 8:12, 16; Heb. 11:17; 12:1-16; I Pet. 1:7; Rev. 2:20 (Convicts us of sin and helplessness) Job 36:8-9, 15; Ps. 119:67; Luke 15:17-18 (Accomplishes God's purposes) Acts 8:3-4; John 9:1-3; 11:3-4; Phil. 1:12ff.; John 13:7; (Returns us to God when we stray); Jud. 4:3; Job 34:31-32; Isa. 10:20; Jer. 31:18; Lam. 2:14-18; Ezek. 14:10-11; Deut. 4:30-31 (Gives us an opportunity to study God's word) Ps. 119:50, 52, 67, 71, 75, 92.

   c. On getting strength and patience:
      Rom. 8:22-27; I Cor. 10:13; Phil. 2:3, 4.
   d. On usefulness in disability or old age:
      Ps. 71:17-18; 92:1-4, 12-15; II Tim. 4:7-8a; Titus 2:2a, 3a.
   e. On sin and how it relates to sickness:
      Ps. 38; 32; (On bitterness) Matt. 5:23-25; 18:21-35; Eph. 4:32 (On a guilty conscience) John 8:9; Acts 23:1; 24:16; I Pet. 3:16 (On confession and forgiveness) Ps. 51; Isa. 1:18; 53:5-6; I John 1:8-10; 2:1.
   f. On God's watchfulness and love:
      (Loneliness) Ps. 25:14-18; Ps. 139; Matt. 28:20; John 14:18; 15:7; Heb. 13:5b; Ps. 34:22b (God's care) Ps. 121; 139; I Pet. 5:7; Ps. 23; 56; Phil. 4:4-7; Rom. 8:25-28, 32, 38-39; Matt. 10:28-31; (Anxiety) Matt. 6:25-34; Ps. 56:3; Josh. 1:9; Ps. 91:15; 5:1-2; Phil. 4;6; Ps. 27:1; Ps. 55:22; Isa. 40:31.

  g. Before an operation:
    Ps. 46:1; 91; Isa. 30:15b; Ex. 33:14; Jer. 32:27; Ezek. 37:6; Matt. 28:20b.
  h. On death and bereavement:
    Dan. 3:16-18; Ps. 23:4; 31:5; John 10:28-29; 11:25-26; 14:1-7; I Thess. 4:13-16; I Cor. 15:51-58; Heb. 14-15.

B. Prayer.
1. When we pray with a sick person, we become a kind of channel to God for him. We help him draw closer to God.
2. Pray:
 a. When anxiety and fear seem high; when there has been frightening news or occurrences.
 b. A little before you actually have to leave. After prayer the person may be in the mood to talk about serious matters. Be ready and have the time available.
3. Pray expressing his feelings and frame of mind. "Lord, it's so easy to be afraid in the face of such news. We tremble at the thought. But you are in our midst, and if the whole world were coming apart in an earthquake, we do not have to be shaken if you are our rock!" Begin in the prayer where the person is. Pray as he would if he could.
4. But then, within the prayer, turn the prayer to the attribute of God which meets the need of the patient. Speak of God's forgiveness to the guilty, of his wisdom to the confused, of his love to the lonely, of his power to the anxious. Begin where he is and take him to where he should be.
5. Pray in simple language.
6. Before praying, ask, "As we go into prayer, is there any request you would especially like me to make?" This can be an excellent conversation starter. Often the person will not begin to talk of serious, personal issues until that question is posed.
7. For the semi-conscious or unconscious, pray loudly, briefly, repetitiously. Use familiar phrases.

C. Relationship.
1. Be warm, interested, friendly, and cheerful (but beware of a phony "breeziness" which in some hospital settings can appear unfeeling).
2. Listen more than you talk. Ask them to talk and focus on their needs and problem. Ask interested questions about subjects they have brought up.

3. Be understanding. Don't jump in with advice before you understand the whole picture.

III. **Guidelines on Procedure**
   A. Preparation.
   1. Learn all you can about the condition of the person physically and emotionally before you go.
   2. Select a Scripture passage on the basis of what you do know of the patient's condition. Reflect on what comments you will make on the text.
   3. Pray for your visit.
   B. Entering.
   1. If you get there during visiting hours, go right to the room. If the door is closed, check first at the nurses' station if it is all right to enter.
   2. If the person is sleeping, ask the nurse if it is all right to awaken him. If not, leave a note.
   3. If the room is crowded with visitors, don't go in.
   4. Sit down, even if the visit is only for a couple of minutes. But don't sit on the bed if possible.
   5. If the sick person is at home, be sure to call before going.
   6. Let the patient be the one to offer to shake hands. If he or she does not do so, don't try.
   C. Conversation.
   1. Be cheerful and remark on how good it is to see them.
   2. Begin with a question: "How is it going?" rather than "How are you feeling?" The latter question may encourage a recital of specific pains.
   3. If the person is well enough to talk, let him do most of the conversation. Listen. If he is too sick or weary, do not burden him by making him carry the conversation. You should do most of the talking and keep the visit very brief in that case.
   4. Seek to find how he is doing spiritually with his condition. Ask questions like: "It's hard facing surgery, isn't it?" etc. Find out if he is experiencing fear, worry, anger, guilt, loneliness, meaninglessness.
   5. Depending on perceived needs, the conversation and the Bible reading could take several turns:
      a. If the patient is recovering, the function of the visit will be to rejoice with him and encourage him to thank God.

b. If the illness is acute or undiagnosed, the function of the visit will be to focus on God's loving care and control of circumstances and stress the need for fellowship with God.
c. If the illness is painful or disabling, it will be necessary to focus on patience and the benefits of affliction.
d. If the illness seems induced or complicated by guilt or disobedience, the visitor must stress with compassion the need for repentance and change.
D. Read the Bible.
E. Pray.
F. Leave appropriate literature: Have an inventory of booklets and tracts and books on the themes of sickness, suffering, worry, discipline. In many cases, the patient will not be able to read, and must be given tapes. Have some devotional guides to always give as a way to encourage prayer and Bible study. Some excellent materials include:

> D.M. Lloyd-Jones, **Spiritual Depression: Causes and Cures** (Chapters can be selected according to need).
> Joni Eareckson, **A Step Further.**
> Jay Adams, **Christ and Your Problems.**
> **What to do About Worry.**

G. LEAVE! Make visits 10-20 minutes long in the hospital, and 20-30 minutes long at home. The more serious the condition, the shorter and the more frequent should be your visits. Watch carefully for signs of fatigue in the patient. Remember, the better you know the patient personally, the longer you will be able to stay without wearying him.
H. After the visit:
1. Pray for God's blessing on what you said and on the patient.
2. Plan for the next visit. Set a time.
3. Evaluate your visit. How did you do? What should you do differently?
4. Contact others in the church who can fill needs that you discovered.

IV. **Miscellaneous Do's and Don'ts**
   A. Do:
   1. Promise to pray for them later (but do it!).
   2. Avoid close contact with contagious persons.
   3. Make presurgery visits the day before.
   4. Be relaxed and strong (not nervous and upset).

5. Adjust your voice and manner to their condition. Speak loudly to some, softly to others.
6. Help in little ways. Get a drink of water, answer the telephone, convey messages, bring items from home.

B. Don't:
1. Talk a lot about your past illnesses.
2. Promise God will heal them. Rather promise that God will be present to bless and hear prayers.
3. Visit when you are sick.
4. Visit during meals. If you are there, insist that they eat as you visit.
5. Guess at diagnosis or second guess the doctor.
6. Criticize the hospital.
7. Ask for too many details about the patient's condition.
8. Relay lots of bad news to them about other people.
9. Whisper to others in the room. Always assume that even apparently unconscious patients can hear you.

FOR FURTHER STUDY:

Sharon Fish and Judith Shelly, **Spiritual Care: The Nurse's Role.**

Andrew Bonar, **The Visitor's Book of Texts.**

PROJECTS:

Interview or have speak to your board a hospital social worker or a Christian medical professional concerning: 1) the social, emotional, and spiritual needs of the hospitalized, 2) what the church is failing to do for the sick, and 3) what the church could do.

Programs for the Handicapped

In order to develop a ministry to persons with a particular physical or mental disability:

I. **Survey hospitals,** public health departments, and other institutions which work with the disabled. Discover if there are any groups of disabled persons in your locale who could benefit from the church's ministry. Look for the mentally retarded, the deaf, the blind, the para- and quadra-plegic, those afflicted with cerebral palsy and muscular dystrophy. These are a few of the largest groupings of disabled persons.

II. **Study about the needs and conditions of persons with the disability.** Information can be usually obtained from a local library. Also write:

    U.S. Department of Health and Human Services
    Bureau of Education for the Handicapped
    U.S. Office of Education
    Washington, D.C. 20202

III. **Conduct a survey and visitation of the homes of the disabled persons to whom you wish to minister. Find these people by:**
    A. The results of the survey.
    B. The ministry/program suggestions which you discover in reading literature. Be sure to contact:

    Joni and Friends
    Box 3225, Woodland Hills, Calif. 91365
    (This is an evangelical organization, formed to help disabled people face their spiritual and emotional problems.)

    National Program for Voluntary Action
    Paramount Building, 1735 "I" St. NW,
    Washington, D.C. 20006
    (Ask for information on working with the physically and mentally handicapped.)

    The organization established for the aid of persons with the disability you are considering. For example: American Foundation for the Blind, the Association for the Deaf, National Paraplegia Foundation, Federation for the Handicapped, Muscular Dystrophy Association of America, United Cerebral Palsy Association, American Occupational Therapy Association, The President's Committee on the Employment of the Handicapped.

    C. The resources of your church.

IV. **Some program ideas will include:**
    A. Trained visitors who know how to show mercy to the retarded and handicapped with regular home visitation, counseling, and support.

B. Christian education and fellowship programs with materials and facilities geared to the needs of the disabled.
C. Many of the services offered to the elderly and the families of the elderly would apply here:
   1. Transportation/escort services.
   2. Home maintenance services.
   3. Helping the disabled person learn a trade.
   4. Staying with the disabled on a regular basis to give family members relief from responsibility.
   5. Classes, counseling, and support groups for parents or family members of the disabled.

FOR FURTHER STUDY:

Lowell G. Colston, **Pastoral Care with Handicapped Persons,** (Fortress).

PROJECT:
1. List all the disabled persons you know. Which of them is handling their disabilities well? Which are not? Interview as many people from the first group that you can. Summarize your findings.
2. Do the survey described above.

Ministry in Disaster

I. **The Need**

In Acts 11:27-30 we read that the prophet Agabus predicted a great famine. In response, the disciples in Antioch decided to provide help for the poor brothers living in Jerusalem.

The early Christians prepared for the relief of natural disaster victims even before the disaster occurred. It would be wonderful if we had prophets to tell us when famines, floods, earthquakes, hurricanes, and tornadoes will strike! And yet, though we cannot know when and where such tragedies will occur, we can be sure that they will. We should then follow the lead of the early Christians and provide for the impending disasters.

II. **The Stages**
   A. Emergency stage (two to six days). People in this stage need to be rescued, to be relocated temporarily, to be given food, to get help in communicating with family and friends, to receive medical help.
   B. Relief stage (twenty to sixty days). People in this stage need to be helped in assessing damage to their home and belongings, to make temporary repairs, to make application to numerous government agencies for help. During this period people need to be shown what their resources are. Delays and administrative snags create a need for encouragement and support. The emotional trauma of what has occurred "comes home." Questions are asked about "what is the purpose in all this?" and "where am I going to live for now?"
   C. Recovery stage (two hundred to six hundred days). People in this stage need permanent repairs and rebuilding of homes. There will be a need for larger loans and grants to finance the work. There is a continued need to help people face and handle grief and anger.

III. **What is needed**
   A. Equipment.
      1. For mobile feeding.
      2. For stationary feeding.
      3. For communication.
      4. For rescue.
      5. For transportation.
      6. For repair, building, cleaning.
   B. Materials.
      1. Clothing.
      2. Bedding.

3. Used furniture.
4. Home building materials.
5. Food supplies.
C. Facilities.
1. For mass shelter.
2. Mobile homes.
3. For stationary feeding.
D. Services.
1. Advocacy (People who do counseling, problem-solving, support, and who help disaster victims find resources and agencies which can meet needs).
2. Home repair/rebuilding skills.
3. Distribution of clothing.
4. Feeding.
5. Clean up of debris.
6. Financial assistance.
7. Counseling.
8. Welfare information service.
9. Setting up a coordination of efforts of all organizations and churches aiding in the disaster response.

IV. **What Your Church Can Do**

No one church or denomination can provide all the equipment, materials, services and facilities needed to respond to a disaster. It is therefore vital for a church to join now in the organizations which meet to coordinate efforts.

A. Contact the American Red Cross in order to obtain training in disaster response for volunteers in the church who can later be called upon to respond to disasters.

B. Contact the National Voluntary Organizations Active in Disaster to see if there is an active chapter in your area. NVOAD acts to coordinate efforts of churches and organizations in disaster response. By entering into discussions with a local chapter, you may be asked to equip your church building to offer certain services in a disaster, or you may be asked to stockpile clothing or food, etc.

C. Contact your denominational committee on Mission to North America. A coordinated Disaster Response Service is being organized in the near future.

Addresses:
American Red Cross
Eastern Headquarters: 615 N. St. Asaph St.
Alexandria, VA 22314
Midwestern Headquarters: 10195 Corporate Sq.
St. Louis, MO 63132
Western Headquarters: 1870 Ogden Dr.
Burlingame, CA 94010

ACTION PLAN

1. What are the most important things which you have learned from this article? List them.

2. Select two or three things which you would like to see put into practice in your church? Name them.

3. In order to implement these, do you need:
   ____ More or better information (about a program, your church, your community, etc.)? What is it?
   ____ More or better skills (abilities, expertise, etc.)? What are they?
   ____ More or better support from key people? Who are they?
   ____ More or better resources (such as money, facilities, personnel, etc.)? What are they?

4. Make a brief plan for securing each of the elements you lack. How could you get information, develop skills, win people's support, raise funds, and so on?

RESOURCES FOR DEACONS

Casework In Diaconal Ministry

Two Kinds of Poverty

When a church confronts a case of need, it is important to recognize that the individual may fall into one of two categories.

His need may have come upon him suddenly. A physical disability, a natural disaster, or unexpected unemployment may have brought him into economic straits, though neither he nor his family have a history of poverty. An example of such a case:

> A young woman, age 28, had recently separated from her husband, who fled to a state where he cannot be forced to support his family. The woman had recently had surgery and has sold her house to pay her medical bills, but is still in need of funds.

On the other hand, a person may come out of a "culture of poverty." Poverty can become a mind-set, a way of life. It can, in a sense, be passed on from one generation to the next. For example, a poor family may have a large number of children, who grow up in crowded and unpleasant conditions, without sufficient parental attention. Such children generally find school disinteresting, since they do poorly in their studies. They may drop out of school early to get married and escape their unhappy home life. But lack of training keeps them in low paying positions. They begin to have children of their own which they cannot support properly. So the cycle continues. Some examples of such cases:

> The husband is 37 and the wife is 36. They both work at minimum wage jobs to care for their eight children (the oldest is 19). Both parents have only fourth grade educations. The oldest daughter needs hospitalization but cannot get good care for lack of funds.

> A young couple married at ages 15 and 16 to escape unhappy home lives. They have two children and are now married just

two years. Their financial needs have been so severe that he pimps for her as a prostitute. Currently their marriage relationship is having problems.

Pastors and workers seeking to help people must recognize that people who are poor in this latter sense need different treatment than people who are "broke." The long term poor will often be cynical and distrustful of authority. They will usually be preoccupied with the present and have little or no concept of "savings," "budgets," and other concepts middle class people take for granted. Their cynicism and despair often inclines them to other poverty-linked habits, such as heavy drinking, gambling, drugs, and crime.

Such people need more than spot relief. They will not always appear grateful. They will not change quickly. Greater patience and care must be taken with them. Education, vocation training, and other counseling will usually be necessary to make any lasting impact on their condition.

DISCUSSION QUESTION:

What problems could be avoided by deacons if these two types of poverty are distinguished?

For further reading: C. Kemp, **Pastoral Care With the Poor,** (New York: Abingdon, 1972).

Assessing Mercy Needs

There are three basic problems that occur frequently in families which have chronic economic problems. Ministers of mercy should look for them immediately.

I. **A Lack of Financial Independence**
   A. **Definition**
      This condition exists when a family cannot generate sufficient income for its needs. There are at least three groups within this category:
      1. Some persons are physically or mentally incapable of working, or working at a job which pays well. This includes many elderly and handicapped persons.
      2. Others are able-bodied, but "emotionally dependent." That is, they have become accustomed to look to other individuals or organizations for income. They are unmotivated to become financially independent.
      3. A third group is able-bodied and emotionally independent (that is, they are uncomfortable with their condition). They have been laid off from their work, or have found their job skills unmarketable or have been saddled with a huge debt.
   B. **Ministry**
      1. Group #1 (the handicapped), need (a) permanent economic-physical aid sufficient to their needs and (b) help to accept their dependent position while maintaining their self-respect.
      2. Group #2 (the able-bodied, emotionally dependent) need (a) to be encouraged/confronted in their psychological dependence. (Discouragement, cynicism and laziness can be helped by giving the persons tasks which are not too hard or too easy, and which produce independence.), (b) to have their vocational aptitudes and skills identified, (c) to learn job seeking skills, (d) to eliminate habits or attitudes that obstruct them from keeping jobs, (e) to help the family find employment opportunities.
      3. Group #3 (the able-bodied, emotionally independent) need all of the help under Group #2, part (1).
   C. **Goal:** When a family has been self-supporting, through income from employment, for at least six months, diaconal aid can cease.

II. **A Lack of Budgetary Control**
   A. **Definition**
      Some economical problems appear, superficially, to be largely

financial dependence, when in fact income is sufficient for needs. Instead, the major problem is a lack of skill in money management. The major indicator of this problem is debt delinquency. If a family has incurred more debts than it is able to pay off consistently (according to contract with creditors), then the family has no budgetary control.

B. **Ministry**

These families need all or some of the following aids:
1. Help to develop efficient shopping skills. Are they impulsive? Taken in by advertisers? Subject to pressure of the children's desires? Unable to find items at reasonable costs?
2. Help to develop realistic priorities for spending. We spend our money on what we think is important to us. But we must reconcile our values with our other needs and income realities. Some people spend due to emotional problems. These must be confronted.
3. Help to develop a financial planning and evaluation system. Can the family draw up and stick to a budget?
4. Help to develop a debt reduction plan. Some outstanding debts (medical expenses, college tuition) place short-term strain on a family's budget. Careful management and financial planning could enable all obligations to be met without increasing income.

C. **Goal.** When a family is able to maintain all payments without delinquency for six months, your ministry to them can be termed "successful." (Note: See **Outline for Financial Counseling** in this manual.)

III. **A Lack of Family Nurture Skills**

A. **Definition**

Behind many economic problems are family problems which make it difficult for parents to seek or keep jobs and maintain budget control. A family must be able to support the efforts of its members in these basic activities. An indicator of this problem is the number of social or legal delinquencies its members have. Also, the school performance of the family's children can be a sign of family nurture.

B. **Ministry**
1. Help to enable family members to communicate (send) desires and thoughts to other members.
2. Help to enable family members to listen to other members.
3. Help to enable family members to establish rules and guidelines for family behaviour. (For parents, this is the ability to set down standards and be consistent in enforcing them.)

4. Help to enable family members to communicate love and concern to one another.
C. **Goal.** Usually, a family's other problems (budgetary control, financial independence) will improve as family nurture improves. Look for a decrease in children's delinquencies or increases in their grades.

Resource: John Guetter, **Service to Families: Problem Solving in Diaconal Outreach.** (Kalamazoo, Mich.: CRWRC, 1981).

Strategies for Adequate Employment

I. **Provide Vocational Counseling**
(See next full article.)

II. **Provide Support Groups for the Unemployed**

A "Job Club" is a group of unemployed or underemployed people. They meet for the purposes of: 1) emotional support and informal peer counseling and 2) learning how to find a job. The importance of these clubs is recognized by anyone who has faced unemployment. It is difficult to stick to job-seeking day in and day out without instruction and support.

The group could be led by members of the congregation. Outside speakers should be brought in to speak on subjects such as conducting a job interview. Deacons should be assigned to each member of the club for encouragement and follow-up. Members of the club should be counseled to eliminate any habits or attitudes which have kept him/her from getting or keeping jobs.

III. **Provide a Job-Seeking Service**

Deacons can actually help the unemployed find jobs by various means:

A. Deacons could develop and maintain a listing of employment opportunities. (This could be anything from full-time jobs to labor for members of the congregation.) Members of the congregation should be encouraged to tell deacons of jobs they know are available, so that the list stays current. Special responsibility would lie with members of the church who are in charge of hiring.

B. Deacons may be able to develop job opportunities.

  a. They may go to a local employer and offer to pay 25% to 50% of a salary so that an unemployed person could work for the business. This incentive gives the employer full-time help for a part-time salary. The deacons could agree to pay the subsidy for a certain period of time. After that the employer is free to terminate if he/she wishes. The advantages of this are: a) it puts the unemployed person to work instead of sitting around feeling useless, b) it provides experience and training for the unemployed person, thus making him more marketable, and c) it often results in a full-time position.

  b. The deacons could start a cooperative, a small business, or industry which could employ a number of unemployed persons. Examples may include a temporary labor pool, home maintenance service, etc.

An Outline For Vocational Counseling

Perhaps the most lasting and appropriate diaconal service to a person is to help him find and keep a good job.

I. Basic Steps for Vocational Counseling
   A. Identify the job skills he has and enjoys using.
      1. Know your "job-skill family" or families.
         a. Manual or mechanical ability. (He works with machines, objects, tools, animals, often outdoors.)
         b. Clerical of numerical ability. (He works with data or figures, usually following other people's instructions.)
         c. Leading or managing ability. (He works with people, organizing them to reach goals.)
         d. Instructing or training ability. (He works with words, knowing how to enlighten, cure, or equip people.)
         e. Analytical or observational ability. (He works with ideas, to research, investigate and solve problems.)
         f. Artistic or intuitive ability. (He works with the imagination, to innovate or create.)
      2. Carefully recollect and examine seven of the most satisfying achievements (or seven of the most satisfying jobs/roles) he has ever done (paid or unpaid). Analyze carefully the skills necessary for each job. Which skills were repeatedly used? (Use "Skills Inventory" on pages 204-222 of Richard Bolles', **What Color is Your Parachute?**)
   B. Identify where he wants to use these skills.
      1. Exclude possibilities.
         a. Geographical areas he can and cannot work in.
         b. Working conditions he can and cannot work in (outdoors/indoors, type of supervisions, number of employees, etc.).
         c. Level of responsibility he can and cannot handle.
         d. Minimum salary for the needs of the family.
      2. Find jobs that use the skills he has. For ideas, check:
         a. **Occupational Outlook Handbook** (1982-83 edition) U.S. Dept. of Labor
            Bureau of Statistics, Bulletin 2200.
         b. Appendix B (pp. 104-115) in Kirk E. Farnsworth, **Life Planning** (Inter-Varsity Press, 1981).

3. Discover organizations in your area that use people with his skills.
    a. Other occupational guides in local libraries.
    b. The yellow pages of the local phone book.
C. **Do "Information Interviewing."**
   Having identified some jobs that "fit" your skills and inclinations, now via the phone book and other information sources, go to the jobs or organizations that interest you and interview them asking:
   1. How did you get into this work?
   2. What do you like best about doing this?
   3. What do you like least about doing this?
   4. Where else can I find people who do this or who are interested in this?
   5. What other kinds of jobs use these same skills (or promote these same ends)?
   6. If they do not know the answer to any of these questions, ask them for the names of someone who does.

   Each interview should lead you to more people in the organization or job you are interested in. You should make them just 15 or 20 minutes long. You should not see yourself as "sneaking in," getting the person to think you are not a job seeker when you really are. You are interested in getting to know the needs and problems of organizations as well as the strengths.
D. **Return to some organizations as job applicant.**
   1. Return to the two or three organizations you like best.
   2. Return to see the person who has the power to hire you (you should know who that is).
   3. Go to them and openly say that you are job-hunting. Explain:
       a. Why you were impressed with the organization.
       b. Why you are interested in the job or line of work.
       c. How your skills can meet needs that you see the organization has.
   4. If there are not job openings now, the employer may hire you, tell you there is one opening shortly, or turn you down. Go to the next place you chose.

Sources: Robert N. Bolles. **What Color is Your Parachute?** (Ten Speed Press, Box 7123, Berkeley, CA 94707). This work is unparalleled in helpfulness and information. To have a person work through it can be formidable for someone with less than a high school education. However, a deacon could use the book to help anyone find a job.

An Outline for Financial Counseling

I. **Determining Where You Are Now**
   A. List monthly expenses after keeping a daily record of *all* expenditures for *at least* 30 days.
      1. Fixed: Tithe, housing, taxes, insurance, other installment payments or dues.
      2. Flexible: Food (in and out), household operation, medical, transportation, utilities, recreation/entertainment, house maintenance, clothing and cleaning, education (school, lessons, books), furniture, gifts, other expenses.
      Note: Beware of *hidden* debts that do not come monthly. Estimate them on a monthly basis. Estimate gifts as well. Also, set aside money for unforeseen medical expenses.
   B. List income each month. Salary, interest and dividends, gifts.
   C. Compare:
      1. Does your income exceed your expenses? Simply keep a record of every expenditure to be sure you maintain budget control.
      2. Do your expenses exceed income? Then you need a debt management program.

II. **Getting Where You Want to Be**
   A. Budget Control.
      1. On the basis of your current expenses and income, set a *realistic* budget for each item on the above list.
      2. Keep a record of every item of income and expense in a ledger. A good example is on pages 50-53 of George L. Ford, **All The Money You Need,** (World Books, 1976) Waco, Texas, 76703.
      3. A good rule of thumb is the 10-75-15 plan. Your goal should be to give 10% of earnings to God's work, use 75% for living expenses, and put 15% of annual earnings into savings and investments.
   B. Debt Management Plan.
      1. Analyze budget problems:
         a. Are financial records and the checkbook being regularly and accurately balanced?
         b. Is there a problem with impulse buying and is it usually done on credit?
         c. Are the housing costs simply too expensive for the family's income?

    d.   Can the amount of money spent on food, household, and automobile be reduced? (See a list of ways to do so on pages 181-195 in Larry Burkett, **Your Finances in Changing Times,** 1975, available from Campus Crusade for Christ, Arrowhead Springs, San Bernadino, CA 92403.)
    e.   Is the family over insured?
    f.   Can the expenses for entertainment and recreation be reduced? (This is nearly always possible!)
2.   Practice a plan to reduce unnecessary buying.
    a.   Buy nothing that is not an absolute necessity (a specifically budgeted item) unless you wait for 30 days.
        1)   When you first desire such an item, record it somewhere with the date.
        2)   Do not buy anything until it is on the list for 30 days.
        3)   Do not ever buy more than one thing on the list in a month.
        4)   Do not use credit cards for anything on the list.
    b.   Before buying anything, ask yourself the questions on this list:
        1)   Can I get along without it?
        2)   Can a less expensive item be substituted?
        3)   Have I compared prices on the same item elsewhere?
        4)   Do I need to use as much?
    c.   Do not go shopping just to browse. Go when you have something specific in mind.
3.   Develop a debt management plan.
    a.   Reduce family living expenses (by decreasing entertainment expenses, impulse buying, housing costs) until 75% of the income covers expenses.
    b.   Put 15% of income into debt liquidation. (This figure is approximate, of course.) When outstanding debts are liquidated, put this 15% into savings and investments. By "outstanding debts" we do not refer to monthly house payments and other such fixed expenses, *unless* payments on these items are behind.
    c.   Give 10% of income to God's work.

How to Help Someone Face Suffering

I. **Admit God's Rights Over Us**
   A. Much of a person's misery in any situation consists of his anger and surprise that the suffering has happened to *him*.
   B. Surprise can be dealt with if a Christian sees from where suffering comes.
      1. John 9:1-5 and Luke 13:1-5 show us that natural disasters and sickness are not usually punishment for particular sins that we have done.
      2. Romans 8:19-23 (cf. Gen. 3:16-18) shows us that the world is filled with disease, death, and natural disasters because of sin in general. It is the curse on the human race.
      3. Therefore, a Christian expects suffering and knows that as part of all sinful mankind he/she deserves it. This diminishes the confusion and surprise when it happens.
   C. Anger can be dealt with if a Christian recognizes God's rights over us.
      1. God created us and sustains us. He owns us. We owe him everything; he owes us nothing (Job 9:12).
      2. Nevertheless, he blesses us far beyond that which we deserve (Ps. 103:4), and if we would ever ask God to be "fair" we would be instantly destroyed. Angry self-pity has no place.

II. **Understand God's Purposes For Us**
   A. He has hidden purposes in everything that happens. Rom. 8:28 — God works all historical circumstances together for your good, if you are a Christian. At the foot of the cross, many people may have thought: "How could God let this good man die? How could God bring any good out of this?" God will work all things together for good, but he does not promise to show exactly how any one incident fits into the complex fabric of history. To try to show us that would be like trying to pour a million gallons of truth into a one ounce brain.
   B. He has revealed purposes in suffering.
      1. In Hebrews 12:1-10 and elsewhere, the Bible teaches us that we should not try to "guess" at God's hidden purposes in tragic incidents, but rather seek his revealed purpose, namely, that we grow in grace.
      2. God uses suffering to:
         a. Break our self-confidence and pride. Suffering doesn't really make us helpless and dependent on

119

God. It just shows us we always have been vulnerable and dependent and forces us to acknowledge the fact.
b. Make us examine ourselves. Suffering and trials will bring out the worst in us. Our weak faith, sharp tongue, laziness, insensitivity to people, worry, bitter spirit, and other weaknesses in character will become evident to us (and others!).
c. Strengthen our loyalty to God. In suffering we will be tempted to rebel against God. In times of health and prosperity, it is easy to obey, but when it costs us to obey, we waver. During trials, we hear God say: "Oh! Were things all right between us as long as I waited on you hand and foot? Now we can see if you are really out to serve me or whether you only expect me to serve you!"
d. Make us more compassionate. When we have suffered, we become more tender-hearted and able to help others in suffering. We become more useful (II Cor. 1:3-4).
e. Enable us to witness for him. The world will be impressed by a Christian's uncomplaining endurance of suffering. They will say, "Well! He must have quite a God to take all this. His God must be real."

III. Grasp God's Perspective on Suffering

We must evaluate suffering by comparing it with eternal glory. Only then will we be able to put suffering in its proper perspective.

A. Balance suffering's duration against eternity. Compared to the endless billions of "years" of eternity without suffering, our troubles are brief. If we think of our lives as only 70 years long, suffering will loom large; if we think of our lives as endless, suffering is a fleeting thing. A billionaire will hardly feel a theft of the $1,000 from his pocket. A middle class man will feel it sorely. Christians are billionaires in glory.

B. Balance suffering's severity against glory. When people tell sufferers that "it's not so bad; it could be worse," they help little. When, instead, we compare our suffering now to the joy and glory of heaven, suffering is "outweighed" (II Cor. 4:17-18). When Stephen caught a glimpse of heaven, he got so excited that he seemed to forget the small matter of his execution (Acts 7:55-56)! One second of glory will outweigh 1000 years of pain.

To get suffering in perspective takes meditation on God's word.

IV. Receive God's Provision for Suffering

A. God promises us that the Spirit will help us in our needs (Rom. 8:26). He cannot help us until we begin to obey. Similarly,

Philippians 2:12-13 tells us God works as we work.

B. In summary, the strength we need for suffering will come in the doing of what responsibilities and duties God requires. Shirk no commands of God. Read, pray, study, fellowship, serve, witness, obey. Do all your duties that you physically can and the God of peace will be with you.

V. **Bible Passages**

Heb. 5:8; 12:1-17; 13:5; Rom. 8:18-30; II Cor. 1:3-12; 4:7-5:5; 11:24-12:10; I Cor. 10:13; Phil. 4:10-15; Matt. 6:25-34; Isa. 43:1-2; Ps. 55:22; Josh. 1:9.

Developing A Ministry Plan

I. **Investigate the Need**

First, reflectively listen. Encourage the person to talk and share their problems and pain. Then, actively approve. Find out how long the problem has existed, what the person has done about it, what has helped it, what has aggravated it, what threat or pressure the person feels most in the situation.

A. What are the *basic causes* of the need? Distinguish between the two kinds of poverty (see article above by the same title).

1. If the person or family you are investigating has the qualities of a person who is "broke-needy," then the deacon's job will be more straightforward.

   a. The basic causes of poverty are: 1) oppression (sinful, unjust treatment by an employer, a landlord, etc.) 2) calamity (sickness, accident, etc.) or 3) sin (poor judgment, laziness, or a lack of self-control, etc.).

   b. The deacon will ordinarily discover one of these causes is at the root of the problem. The deacons should 1) meet the immediate need, 2) seek to attack the root of the need. For example, find a new job, get medical attention, repent of the sin and get counseling, and so on.

2. If the person or family being investigated has the qualities of a person who is from a background of chronic poverty, then the family will not have one basic cause at the root of their need. Rather, all three causes of poverty listed above will be present and intertwined tightly. There may be a heavy attitude of pessimism and no sense of "savings," "budgeting" or other concepts obvious to middle class people. Helping such a family will take long term aid.

B. Which of the three ordinary sub-problems are present? (See article above "Assessing Mercy Needs" page 111.)

1. Insufficient income for needs (unemployment or underemployment).

   a. Is the person physically dependent?
   b. Emotionally dependent?
   c. Physically and emotionally independent?

2. Lack of budgetary control (sufficient income but lack of skill in money management).

   a. Due to inefficient shopping skills?
   b. Due to unrealistic priorities?
   c. Due to unexpected expenses?

  d. Due to lack of discipline?
 3. Lack of family nurture skills?
C. What is the *exact extent* of the need?
 1. What is the extent of the financial need?
  a. What are the total assets?
  b. What is the total income?
  c. What are the expenses and liabilities? Outstanding debts?
  d. What are the other resources available: e.g. family? friends? government and private agencies with funds for which this family is eligible? church members who may have an interest in helping?
 2. What other specific problems are related to the financial?
  a. Health problems and disabilities.
  b. Educational, recreational and social needs going unmet.
  c. Legal problems.
  d. Interpersonal or emotional problems besides a lack of family nurture skills.
 3. What is the family's spiritual state?
  a. Are they Christian?
  b. Are they related to a church?
D. Make a brief list of all the problems you have found:
 1. Root causes.
 2. Sub-problems.
 3. Extent of financial need: the figures.
 4. All other related problems.

II. Outline the Problem

A. Nearly all the problems can be divided into four basic types.
 1. Inadequate information. Some problems require educational counseling. The person is simply unaware of how to apply for a job, how to save money, where to get medical help or other services. The basic need is for instruction.
 2. Inadequate support system. Some problems are caused or aggravated by a lack of relationships which are supportive of responsible behavior. If family or friends are unsympathetic and unhelpful a person may need more than information. He needs relationships.
 3. Inadequate abilities. Some problems go deeper than knowledge lack and support systems. A person may lack the skills

and proficiency to do some things, such as manage money, communicate clearly, have a marketable job skill, etc. The need is for training.
4. Inadequate material resources. A person who lacks adequate income, housing, clothing, and food lacks material resources. Though this problem is often the result of one of the other three sub-problems, a lack of material resources can also be the result of natural disaster, and so on. It may be the only problem the person has.

B. Now state each problem in words which are specific and which define the person's responsibility. For example: "You cannot resolve conflicts on the job without anger and this has cost you your last two jobs" and "Your rent has increased 50% in the last year while your salary has only increased 5%."

C. Take the problem statements to the person and seek to reach an agreement on each one through discussion.

III. Outline A Solution

A. Choose an order in which to tackle the problems. Which problem seems to be more fundamental than the others? Remember your look at root causes at the beginning of the investigation. Ask the person his opinion. Decide together.

B. Set a goal or goals for each problem. The goal is a specific statement of what you wish the condition to be after the problem is "solved" and when you wish it to be solved. (This way, both you and the person in need know exactly where you are headed.) Examples of goals: "By September to have all bills paid except _____, and by November to have no outstanding debts."

C. Brainstorm all possible alternatives to reach the goal. Add up the pros and cons of each. Allow the person to help in choosing an alternative unless his choice is dangerous or unbiblical.

D. When alternatives are chosen, write up a ministry plan, including:
  1. The form of the help.
     a. Financial help from the deacons' funds? Loan? One cash gift? Payments to the person or the direct payment of bills?
     b. Financial help from concerned individuals coordinated by the deacons?
     c. Work and service of church members (such as baby sitting, legal advice, repair work to a home, moving, etc.). This sort of help offered free can speed up debt liquidation and a balanced budget.
     d. Payment "in kind" (food, clothing, furniture)?

       e. Other help from secular agencies?
       f. Job training and placement? Other education, paid for by the church?
  2. The conditions for continued help.
       a. Financial counseling? Will the family be asked to work on a budget, worked out in consultation with deacons?
       b. Personal counseling? Will the person agree to see personal or interpersonal problems are involved in the economic need?
  3. The ministry to the spiritual condition.
       a. The ministering deacons should always explain the motivation behind the help as their experience of the grace of God. The gospel must be shared with the person at some point during the helping relationship, if the person is not a Christian, or if his/her spiritual condition is unknown to you.
       b. If the person is a Christian, there should be a plan drawn up to help him or her grow in grace during this trial, to help him or her look at suffering from a biblical perspective, and to involve him in the worship and fellowship of the church.

E. Make a plan to evaluate your ministry's effectiveness by judging progress toward goals.

RESOURCES:

John Guetter, **Service to Families: Problem-Solving Skills in Diaconal Outreach** (Kalamazoo: Michigan, CRWRC, 1981).

Two Case Studies

Case A

Two lay people from your church are visiting in the homes of children who attended the Vacation Bible School. In one home, they find Mrs. C. (who is about 32) living with her four children (ages 16, 13, 11, 7). The oldest girl has twin baby girls (age 1). Mrs. C. has been married three times, has been divorced twice, and does not know where her present husband is. She can barely provide for the family. Mrs. C. has only a third-grade education and cannot hold any well-paying jobs. She is currently out of work. Daughter Joan shows positive interest in spiritual things and has a lengthy discussion about the gospel. But Joan then tells her friends that both she and her mother supplement their incomes through prostitution. "If I stop that now, Mom'll be mad and then we won't be able to eat!"

Case B

A family in the church has bought an expensive home. The couple, Fred and Monica, were counting on both their incomes to continue for several years. But, shortly after the purchase of the house, Monica found herself with a surprise pregnancy. Also Fred developed a kidney problem and was out of work for six months. Fred is now all right, and the baby has just been born; now Monica has decided not to go back to work, but wishes to stay home with the child.

All this has put them in economic straits. They cannot meet the house payments and have gotten some months behind. They are trying to sell the house, but the real estate people warn that they need to do some painting and renovating before it will sell. Fred goes to the deacons and says, "Could we get the deacons to come and help us paint and do some repairs to the house? We can't afford to get it done any other way!" When another deacon hears of the request, he is disgruntled. "Fred's house is twice the size of mine and he has a better paying job than me. Why should I be helping him?"

DIRECTIONS:

1. Refer to two previous articles: "Two Common Objectives to Mercy Ministry" page 21 and "Five Common Questions on Evaluating Need" page 23.
   What biblical principles apply to each case?
2. Refer to the article: "Writing a Ministry Plan."
   a. Evaluate in each case the problems and needs according to the outline in Part I of the Ministry Plan.
   b. Form a plan for helping the families in each case according to the outline in Part II of the Ministry Plan.

ACTION PLAN

1. What are the most important things which you have learned from this article? List them.

2. Select two or three things which you would like to see put into practice in your church? Name them.

3. In order to implement these, do you need:
   ____ More or better information (about a program, your church, your community, etc.)? What is it?
   ____ More or better skills (abilities, expertise, etc.)? What are they?
   ____ More or better support from key people? Who are they?
   ____ More or better resources (such as money, facilities, personnel, etc.)? What are they?

4. Make a brief plan for securing each of the elements you lack. How could you get information, develop skills, win people's support, raise funds, and so on?